Fracking

by Kevin Hillstrom

LUCENT BOOKS
A part of Gale, Cengage Learning

Detroit • New York • San Francisco • New Haven, Conn • Waterville, Maine • London

LIBRARY OF CONGRESS CATALOGING-IN-PUBLICATION DATA

Hillstrom, Kevin, 1963-
Fracking / by Kevin Hillstrom.
    pages cm. -- (Hot topics)
Includes bibliographical references and index.
ISBN 978-1-4205-0869-7 (hardcover)
1. Shale gas reservoirs--United States--Popular works. 2. Hydraulic fracturing--Government policy--United States--Popular works. I. Title.
TN881.A1H55 2013
622'.3381--dc23

                                                    2012038771

Lucent Books
27500 Drake Rd.
Farmington Hills, MI 48331

ISBN-13: 978-1-4205-0869-7
ISBN-10: 1-4205-0869-5

Printed in the United States of America
3 4 5 6 7 17 16 15 14

CONTENTS

FOREWORD 4

INTRODUCTION 6
The Promise and Peril of Fracking

CHAPTER 1 8
The Origins and Development of Fracking

CHAPTER 2 25
How Modern Fracking Works

CHAPTER 3 35
The Benefits of Fracking

CHAPTER 4 52
The Drawbacks of Fracking

CHAPTER 5 68
Fracking in the Twenty-First Century

NOTES 79

DISCUSSION QUESTIONS 85

ORGANIZATIONS TO CONTACT 87

FOR MORE INFORMATION 89

INDEX 91

PICTURE CREDITS 95

ABOUT THE AUTHOR 96

FOREWORD

Young people today are bombarded with information. Aside from traditional sources such as newspapers, television, and the radio, they are inundated with a nearly continuous stream of data from electronic media. They send and receive e-mails and instant messages, read and write online "blogs," participate in chat rooms and forums, and surf the web for hours. This trend is likely to continue. As Patricia Senn Breivik, the former dean of university libraries at Wayne State University in Detroit, has stated, "Information overload will only increase in the future. By 2020, for example, the available body of information is expected to double every 73 days! How will these students find the information they need in this coming tidal wave of information?"

Ironically, this overabundance of information can actually impede efforts to understand complex issues. Whether the topic is abortion, the death penalty, gay rights, or obesity, the deluge of fact and opinion that floods the print and electronic media is overwhelming. The news media report the results of polls and studies that contradict one another. Cable news shows, talk radio programs, and newspaper editorials promote narrow viewpoints and omit facts that challenge their own political biases. The World Wide Web is an electronic minefield where legitimate scholars compete with the postings of ordinary citizens who may or may not be well-informed or capable of reasoned argument. At times, strongly worded testimonials and opinion pieces both in print and electronic media are presented as factual accounts.

Conflicting quotes and statistics can confuse even the most diligent researchers. A good example of this is the question of whether or not the death penalty deters crime. For instance, one study found that murders decreased by nearly one-third when the death penalty was reinstated in New York in 1995. Death penalty supporters cite this finding to support their argument that the existence of the death penalty deters criminals from committing murder. However, another study found that states without the death penalty have murder rates below the national average. This study is cited by opponents of capital punishment, who reject the claim that the death penalty deters murder. Students need context and clear, informed discussion if they are to think critically and make informed decisions.

The Hot Topics series is designed to help young people wade through the glut of fact, opinion, and rhetoric so that they can think critically about controversial issues. Only by reading and thinking critically will they be able to formulate a viewpoint that is not simply the parroted views of others. Each volume of the series focuses on one of today's most pressing social issues and provides a balanced overview of the topic. Carefully crafted narrative, fully documented primary and secondary source quotes, informative sidebars, and study questions all provide excellent starting points for research and discussion. Full-color photographs and charts enhance all volumes in the series. With its many useful features, the Hot Topics series is a valuable resource for young people struggling to understand the pressing issues of the modern era.

INTRODUCTION

THE PROMISE AND PERIL OF FRACKING

Over the last century the lives of billions of people around the world have been fundamentally transformed by new machines and technologies—and by the quest for energy sources to power the equipment and innovations of the evolving industrial age. Those power sources have included fossil fuels like oil and coal, as well as nuclear energy and hydroelectric energy from dams. More recently, scientists, entrepreneurs, and policy makers have invested heavily in sophisticated "green" technologies designed to harness the power of the wind and the sun.

Another fossil fuel—natural gas—has also been a part of the energy picture in the United States and other advanced nations. As recently as a decade ago, though, it only provided a small fraction of the world's total energy needs. At that time, consumers and energy companies had no reason to think that gas would ever become anything more than a modest supporting player.

The status of natural gas changed in the late 1990s and early 2000s, as scientists and engineers came up with a new technique for unlocking huge reserves of natural gas deep under the earth's surface. They called this technique hydraulic fracturing—"fracking," for short—and energy companies quickly rushed forward to employ it at locations all across the United States. By 2008 fracking had sent production of inexpensive and clean-burning natural gas so high that scientists, lawmakers, environmentalists, and industry executives were openly predicting that the world was on the verge of entering a "golden age of gas."

Around this same time fracking's reputation began to fray. A rising tide of news stories and academic studies warned of unwelcome side effects from this new method of gas extraction. "The gallons of chemicals used for drilling could, potentially, contaminate nearby drinking wells," wrote environmental reporter Brad Plumer. "The disposal of wastewater [from fracking] has been linked to earthquakes in places like Ohio. And there's the possibility that methane leaks from fracking could make natural gas even worse for global warming than coal. That, in turn, has led to a prickly debate over how fracking should be regulated."[1]

This debate has grown progressively more bitter. Fracking supporters accuse opponents of needlessly scaring citizens with exaggerated tales of polluted drinking water and poisoned air. Opponents accuse the natural gas industry and other fracking advocates of downplaying the extent of the technique's problems in order to make money. Many Americans who hear these conflicting messages are not sure what to believe. In addition, large numbers of Americans remain completely unfamiliar with the fracking controversy, despite its potentially sizable impact on energy, the environment, and public health. A 2012 survey conducted by the University of Texas, for example, found that 35 percent of people in the United States had "never heard of" the process, while another 28 percent "were not familiar" with it. In other words, nearly two out of three Americans still do not really know what the fracking process is. "Fracking is a case," concluded pollster Sheril Kirshenbaum, "where the public lags behind the science and the technology, so we are left with a highly controversial topic that few Americans understand. But this technology is not only a big deal; it's already changing the international energy landscape."[2] This volume is an effort to inform readers about fracking technology, its benefits and drawbacks, and its growing impact on American society.

The Origins and Development of Fracking

During the course of the nineteenth century, the United States and other nations around the world were forever changed by the Industrial Revolution. This mighty wave of technological and mechanical advances altered the economic, political, social, and environmental fabric of daily life in numerous ways. In America and elsewhere, households, communities, and states that had long depended on primitive systems of farming for their economic health and vitality turned to huge factories; vast rail, water, and road transport systems; and powerful machines for sustenance. This evolution in scientific and technical knowledge enabled entrepreneurs and investors not only to develop major new industries but also to transform existing industries. Farming operations that had depended for many generations on the muscle power of humans and horses, for example, were transformed by mechanical threshers, combines, and milking machines by the early twentieth century.

The daily experiences of men, women, and children in the United States and other industrializing nations underwent dramatic changes as well. Complex systems of electrification were introduced in homes, department stores, and entire towns. People became accustomed to keeping the nighttime at bay through the flip of a light switch, and as the twentieth century unfurled, they acquired all kinds of convenient or entertaining machines and devices that could be powered simply by plugging them into an electrical socket. Radios, televisions, hair dryers, blenders, clothes dryers, refrigerators, and microwave ovens all became standard features in American homes. The electrification of society, in other words, brought the modern world into existence. "Without a reliable supply of electricity, we couldn't use the lightweight, powerful electric motors that make elevators possible," observed the National Academy of Engineering.

> Without elevators, skyscrapers wouldn't exist—and the dramatic skylines of the world's major metropolises would be considerably more modest. Without a reliable supply of electricity, kidney dialysis machines and other life support equipment would be useless to the many patients who depend on them. Without electricity to power traffic lights, the commute to and from work would be mayhem—or maybe not. Without electricity to power automobile factories, we wouldn't have streets and highways full of automobiles either.[3]

Sources of Fuel for the Modern World

The development of electricity sparked the creation of an assortment of new industries dedicated to providing the energy necessary to keep the lights on in kitchens, factories, shops, airports, and military bases in America and around the world. These industries emerged as scientists, inventors, and engineers learned how to convert the world's natural resources into energy. The most important of the energy sources were so-called fossil fuels like coal and oil, both of which were extracted from vast underground deposits that seemed to be of inexhaustible size. People also learned how to harness the power of rivers through hydroelectric dams.

These energy innovations vaulted the United States to a leading position among nations, both in terms of its economic power and its standard of living. At the same time, though, America's demand for energy increased dramatically. By the mid-1950s the United States was consuming more than one-third of all the energy being produced worldwide, and the average American was using six times as much energy as an average citizen of any other country. "We were using that energy to produce more goods and wealth, to be sure, but we were also simply using more energy, to heat our homes, cool our offices, and above all, drive our cars,"[4] wrote environmental historian Paul Roberts.

The Forgotten Fossil Fuel

Around this same time, another fossil fuel known as natural gas emerged as an energy resource. Like coal and oil, natural gas is formed when decayed vegetation and animal matter is subjected to subterranean heat and pressure from layers of rock over many millennia. Unlike coal and oil, though, it remained only a minor contributor to the world's energy picture well into the twentieth century.

A NEW WORLD OF OPPORTUNITY

"Energy affects all aspects of American life and is indispensable for economic growth. The hydraulic fracturing process is opening up new opportunities to access affordable and reliable energy in this country. State legislatures and the federal government are recognizing this opportunity and will hopefully allow the industry to flourish in a responsible manner." —Todd Wynn, director of the Energy, Environment, and Agriculture Task Force of the American Legislative Exchange Council

Quoted in H. Sterling Burnett. "Kansas Cashing In on Fracking." *Heartlander*, February 1, 2012. http://news.heartland.org/newspaper-article/2012/02/01/kansas-cashing-fracking.

Inventor Robert Bunsen had proved that natural gas could be used for cooking and heating purposes back in the 1850s. Transporting the gaseous fuel to market, though, posed a much greater challenge than did coal (which came in solid form) or oil and its chief by-products, kerosene and gasoline (all of which came in liquid form). As a result, natural gas sales were mostly limited to cities that used the fuel for their street lamps. Even there, though, natural gas was nudged to the energy sidelines in the late 1800s, when cities invested heavily in electrical power grids that ran on coal and oil.

Natural gas remained mostly forgotten for the next several decades. As writer Seamus McGraw noted, it came to be seen as "a useful fuel for cooking, perhaps for heating a few homes, but not much else."[5] The perceived value of gas declined to the point that many oil companies just burned the material off

Traffic jams are a common sight on freeways in Los Angeles, California, and across the United States, where the car-dependent American lifestyle results in the consumption of large amounts of gasoline.

during the drilling process. "Natural gas was the orphan of the oil industry," wrote energy expert Daniel Yergin. "The problem was transmission: how to get it to the markets in the Northeast and the Midwest, where both the large populations and the major industries of the country were to be found."[6]

In the 1940s and 1950s, though, American lawmakers and energy industry executives gave natural gas a second look. In 1942, for example, President Franklin D. Roosevelt sent a letter to Secretary of the Interior Harold Ickes, who was responsible for overseeing drilling and mining operations on America's publicly owned lands. "I wish you would get some of your people to look into the possibility of using natural gas," declared Roosevelt. "I am told that there are a number of fields in the West and the Southwest where practically no oil has been discovered but where an enormous amount of natural gas is lying idle in the ground because it is too far to pipe to large communities."[7]

The resurgence of interest in natural gas stemmed from several factors. One was World War II, which greatly increased the energy needs of U.S. factories that were working around the clock to build airplanes, tanks, trucks, rifles, clothing, bandages, and other supplies for the war effort. Energy industry veterans of this era also came to realize that gradual improvements in pipeline manufacturing and welding technology made the notion of building vast natural gas pipeline systems across America more realistic than ever before.

Finally, the United States came to the alarming realization that it no longer had enough domestic oil reserves—oil that it could extract from its own land and coastal waters—to meet its enormous energy appetite. This discovery was made even more chilling by the fact that the problem was worsening with each passing year due to soaring consumption of gasoline, a major oil derivative. Gasoline consumption skyrocketed in part because Americans genuinely enjoyed driving their automobiles and trucks. But the rapid increase also stemmed from political choices that made Americans heavily dependent on their cars. State and federal authorities invested primarily in new roads, bridges, and highways rather than mass-transit rail and bus systems. In addition, most new home construction took place in suburbs that were far away from urban centers. As a result, millions of Americans needed their cars to take them to and from work, school, and the grocery store on a regular basis.

The Development of Hydraulic Fracturing

During the course of the 1940s, American energy companies devoted growing amounts of money and attention to natural gas. By 1950 the United States had emerged as the clear global leader in natural gas drilling, accounting for about 90 percent of total

A pipeline crosses the terrain in New York State in the early 1950s, when the United States accounted for 90 percent of global natural gas production.

world production. Most of these operations exploited easily accessible natural gas deposits, some of which could be extracted in tandem with underground oil or coal reserves. As the years passed by and the number of these easily tapped gas resources began to dwindle, however, natural gas companies expressed increased interest in "shale gas"—natural gas deposits imprisoned in underground shale rock formations.

The big problem with shale gas was that it was very difficult to unlock and retrieve. During the second half of the twentieth century, however, scientists and engineers around the world developed a technology called hydraulic fracturing—commonly known as "fracking." This practice involves pumping millions of gallons of highly pressurized water, sand, and chemicals into subterranean shale formations until the fine-grained shale breaks open. At that point, the natural gas (and sometimes oil) trapped within the rock is released and flows toward the earth's surface, where it can be more easily gathered up.

Fracking methods had actually been used on a limited basis as far back as the 1860s, when American oil companies tried a primitive version of the practice in an effort to reach oil deposits in Pennsylvania, New York, and West Virginia. These early efforts to break open rock formations relied heavily on gunpowder and nitroglycerin, an explosive liquid that was notoriously unstable. Fracking did not become a widespread practice, though, and over time the industry turned its attention to less dangerous oil and gas retrieval methods. Fracking eventually came to be seen as a relic of the energy industry's early days, not a viable tool for modern companies.

This viewpoint rapidly changed in the late 1940s and 1950s, however, as energy companies pivoted back toward natural gas. In 1947 the Stanolind Oil and Gas Corporation carried out an experimental fracking operation on a field in Kansas. Two years later the Halliburton Oil Well Cementing Company carried out the first commercial application of hydraulic fracturing on underground deposits in Oklahoma and Texas. These successes not only established fracking as an effective tool for gas and oil exploration, they also placed Halliburton in a dominant position in the industry. Halliburton has remained a major force in hydraulic fracturing and fossil fuel exploration ever since.

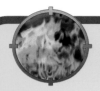

Early Fracking Employed Nitroglycerin

During the nineteenth century, American oil companies sometimes relied on dangerous tactics to break up underground rock formations that blocked them from accessing fossil fuel deposits. One common practice was to lower nitroglycerin into open wells and then detonate the explosive liquid. Nitroglycerin sometimes succeeded in fracturing rock formations so that oil would be released. But the unstable chemical also caused a lot of oil field casualties. "A flame or a spark would not explode Nitro-Glycerin readily," wrote nineteenth-century oil industry historian John J. McLaurin, "but the chap who struck it a hard rap might as well avoid trouble among his heirs by having had his will written and a cigar-box ordered to hold such fragments as his weeping relatives could pick from the surrounding district."

Quoted in American Oil and Gas Historical Society. "Shooters—a 'Fracking' History." http://aoghs.org/technology/shooters-well-fracking-history.

During the second half of the twentieth century, fracking slowly spread to many other parts of the world. The Soviet Union, which held vast underground reservoirs of natural gas, carried out its first hydraulic fracturing operation in 1952. Other countries with natural gas reserves followed suit, including Algeria, Austria, Belgium, Bulgaria, Czechoslovakia, France, Germany, Hungary, Italy, the Netherlands, Poland, Romania, and the United Kingdom.

Meanwhile, big energy consumers like the United States and Japan continued to show interest in reducing their dependence on oil and coal. Their desire to diversify was sparked by events like the 1973 Arab oil embargo, in which major oil producers in the Middle East drastically raised the global price of oil. But it also arose in response to accumulating evidence that oil and coal consumption was taking a heavy environmental toll on air quality, land and water resources, and wildlife. As a result, the United States, Japan, France, and other countries poured money into oil and coal alternatives like natural gas, nuclear power, and solar power.

Fracking Boosts the Natural Gas Industry

In the 1970s and 1980s, the U.S. government worked closely with American energy companies to further develop hydraulic fracturing technology. These research efforts produced two major breakthroughs that made fracking more economical and enabled users to apply the technology much more frequently. First, oil and gas companies learned during the 1980s and early 1990s how to drill horizontally through thick layers of rock to reach previously unreachable deposits. Second, in the late 1990s industry engineers developed an extremely effective type of fracturing fluid known as "slickwater." This fluid was composed of high volumes of water and limited amounts of sand and chemicals. The move to slickwater, which adds chemicals to water in order to increase its flow rate—and thus its shattering impact on underground shale formations that hold natural gas—quickly spread across the entire industry.

To many lawmakers and people involved in the energy industry, these refinements to hydraulic fracturing operations came in the nick of time. In 1993 the monetary value of the natural gas produced in the United States had actually surpassed the value of the oil produced domestically for the first time. As its value rose, many industry observers expressed fears that the country would soon exhaust its natural gas supplies. The rise of fracking dispelled these worries because it gave companies the means to unlock enormous volumes of shale gas that had been beyond the reach of previous generations.

Before long, fracking operations were being put into place or expanded over the Barnett Shale field in Texas, the Bakken Shale in North Dakota, and other big shale formations that had been identified in the Rocky Mountains, the Gulf Coast region, and the Midwest. The shale field that eventually drew the most attention, though, was the Marcellus Shale, which extends from West Virginia through Pennsylvania all the way to New York State. "This gas-trapping shale formation has been estimated to hold as much gas as the whole United States consumes in a century," wrote environmental journalist Bill McKibben. "The gas is also ideally situated along the route of many existing natural gas pipelines and near the heavy-consumption eastern megalopolis

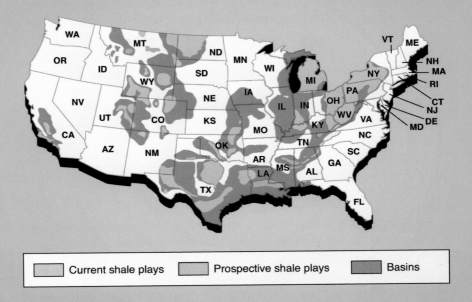

Main Shale Deposits in the United States

| Current shale plays | Prospective shale plays | Basins |

Taken from: www.energyindustryphotos.com/shale_gas_map_shale_basins.htm.

[chain of large cities]. If you're an energy company, it's about the best place on the planet to find a huge pool of gas."[8]

Fracking boosted the production of shale gas in the United States by 17 percent from 2000 to 2006. Natural gas from shale jumped from 2 percent to 6 percent of all domestic natural gas production during this same period. Natural gas production from hydraulic fracturing did not truly begin soaring, though, until after 2006, when several controversial provisions of the Energy Policy Act of 2005 went into effect.

The Halliburton Loophole

The Energy Policy Act of 2005 was a comprehensive energy bill passed by Congress and signed into law by President George W. Bush. Much of the bill was crafted by Vice President Dick Cheney—a former energy industry executive whose positions included chair and CEO of Halliburton from 1995 to 2000—and oil- and gas-industry executives in private White House meetings. The act exempted Halliburton and other companies that engaged in fracking from having to follow major provisions of some of the country's most important environmental laws, including the Safe Drinking Water Act and the Clean Water Act.

The environmental exemptions granted to fracking companies concerned many environmental, wilderness conservation, and public health activists and scientists. "Excluding the natural gas industry from these important protections puts our air and water at serious risk,"[9] said a spokesperson for the Sierra Club, one of America's best-known environmental organizations. Critics emphasized that the exemptions, which they derisively called the "Halliburton Loophole," gave gas companies the legal right

President George W. Bush signs the Energy Policy Act of 2005, which exempted companies engaged in fracking from certain environmental laws.

to use all sorts of potentially toxic chemicals in their slickwater mixtures. Environmentalists and public health advocates warned that if these chemicals escaped into underground lakes of drinking water (known as aquifers) or surface rivers and lakes, they could endanger human life and area ecosystems.

AN UNFAIR LOOPHOLE

"While the average citizen can receive harsh punishment under federal law for dumping a car battery into a pond, gas companies, thanks to what has become known as the Halliburton Loophole, are allowed to pump millions of gallons of fluid containing toxic chemicals into the ground, right next to our aquifers, without even having to identify them." —Journalist Christopher Bateman

Christopher Bateman. "A Colossal Fracking Mess." *Vanity Fair*, June 21, 2010. www .vanityfair.com/business/features/2010/06/fracking-in-pennsylvania-201006.

Despite these worries, however, some environmental organizations and activists expressed cautious support for shale gas. They saw clean-burning natural gas as a promising "green energy" replacement for oil and especially coal, which had long been the dominant fuel for America's electricity-generating power plants. "Coal is neither cheap nor clean," declared prominent environmentalist Robert F. Kennedy Jr., who issued a public statement of support for fracking and shale gas in 2009.

Ozone and particulates from coal plants kill tens of thousands of Americans each year and cause widespread illnesses and disease. Acid rain [from coal consumption] has destroyed millions of acres of valuable forests and sterilized one in five Adirondack lakes. Neurotoxic mercury raining from these [coal-fired] plants has contaminated fish in every state and poisons over a million American women and children annually. Coal industry strip mines have already destroyed 500 mountains in Appalachia [and] buried 2,000 miles of rivers and streams. . . . Finally, coal, which supplies 46 percent of our electric power, is the most important source of America's greenhouse gases [that contribute to global climate change].[10]

Growing Reliance on Shale Gas

Shale gas obtained through fracking technology continued to increase during the first decade of the twenty-first century. The number of drilling permits issued in Pennsylvania alone jumped from 122 in 2007 to 3,337 in 2011, according to the Marcellus Center for Outreach and Research at Penn State University. From 2006 to 2010 total shale gas production in the United States jumped almost fivefold, skyrocketing from 1.0 trillion cubic feet to 4.8 trillion cubic feet (28 billion cu. m to 136 billion cu. m) annually. By 2010 shale gas had grown to account for 23 percent of the nation's total natural gas supply—and U.S. energy officials predicted that it would account for nearly half of the total U.S. natural gas supply by 2035. An energy industry group called the National Petroleum Council issued a similar forecast. The council predicted that 60 to 80 percent of natural gas wells drilled across America from 2010 to 2020 would use fracking techniques.

The infusion of shale gas obtained through fracking had many positive economic benefits for Americans. As the supply of natural gas increased, the price of the fuel dropped significantly. This was a welcome development to millions of American families and business owners who saw their heating and electric bills drop. Fracking supporters also emphasized that the technology boosted regional employment and provided local communities with additional tax revenue for schools and other needs. A 2010 paper from the American Petroleum Institute, for example, claimed that Marcellus Shale fracking operations created forty-four thousand new jobs in Pennsylvania in 2009 alone. The report also estimated that the operations added $389 million in state and local revenue, over $1 billion in federal tax revenue, and almost $4 billion in value to the state's overall economy. In his 2012 State of the Union address, President Barack Obama suggested that hydraulic fracturing could create up to six hundred thousand American jobs by the end of the decade.

During this same period, though, reports of environmental and public health problems associated with fracking greatly increased. Numerous stories and investigations alleged that fracking operations were contaminating water supplies, destroying

Workers move a section of well casing into place at a fracking site in Burlington, Pennsylvania. Supporters cite new jobs and an overall boost to the local economies as benefits of shale oil drilling practices.

rural landscapes, and contributing to global climate change to a much greater degree than previously believed. Critics warned that if the natural gas industry and state and federal officials did not do a better job of protecting the environment and safeguarding the health of local communities, public support for fracking would plummet. "[Fracking companies] have derailed the kind of strong, rigorous regulation needed to safely extract and deploy gas-generated power and earn public credibility and trust," stated Kennedy, who in 2012 renounced his previous support for shale gas drilling. "My current position is that I oppose shale gas extraction by means of fracking unless and until the industry can prove it CAN and WILL be done safely for both human health and the environment."[11]

Controversy over the Term *Fracking*

The natural gas industry and its defenders rejected charges that hydraulic fracturing jeopardized the health and well-being of

The Importance of Sand to Fracking

Most of the controversy surrounding hydraulic fracturing concerns the high volumes of water and the toxic chemicals used in the process. The third ingredient in slickwater, though, is also important. Sand acts as a proppant—a substance that keeps fractures open so that natural gas and oil can seep out of shale formations and be harvested. According to U.S. energy industry statistics, 6.5 million tons of American sand were mined, washed, processed, transported to well sites, and injected into the earth as part of domestic fracking operations in 2009 alone. This amount is equivalent to the weight of Egypt's Great Pyramid of Giza, the oldest of the so-called Seven Ancient Wonders of the World.

Americans. They insisted that fracking was safe and environmentally friendly and that opposition to the practice was based on misunderstandings and hysteria. They also said that the industry was dedicated to improving well construction and other aspects of fracking in order to make sure that their operations remained as safe as possible.

These assurances failed to defuse the controversy over fracking, however. To the contrary, the showdown over hydraulic fracturing intensified. Natural gas companies and other pro-fracking voices launched expensive public relations campaigns that sought to reassure the American public that the practice was safe and economically beneficial. Opponents, meanwhile, shone a spotlight on American families and communities that they claimed had been devastated by the unintended environmental and health consequences of fracking.

This dispute became so bitter that even the term *fracking* became mired in controversy. Back in the 1980s the word—and the way it was spelled—was not a source of hard feelings. *Fracking*, in fact, was commonly used in energy industry trade journals and press releases throughout the decade as a shorthand version of "hydraulic fracturing." As time passed, however, some people within the drilling industry began spelling the word without the *k*—that is, *fraccing* or *fracing*. Others expressed a preference for the full phrase "hydraulic fracturing."

This change in attitude has been traced in part to the science-fiction television series *Battlestar Galactica* (2004–2009), which made heavy use of the word *frack* as a substitute for a well-known real curse word that begins with the letter *f*. Since then the negative connotations of *frack* have been blamed on environmental activists—sometimes called "fracktivists"—who seized on the coarse-sounding word and

A woman makes her feelings about shale gas drilling known at an anti-fracking rally in New York in 2012.

learned to employ it with scorn. "It was created by the industry, and the industry is going to have to live with it,"[12] said Kate Sinding, an attorney who works on drilling issues for the Natural Resources Defense Council.

Members of the natural gas industry reluctantly agreed. They admitted that the term had become so familiar that even pro-drilling news media outlets used it when covering natural gas stories. Given this reality, most hydraulic fracturing advocates seemed resigned to the idea that the word *fracking* is here to stay.

How Modern Fracking Works

The process of hydraulic fracturing has progressed greatly in the United States since it was first used for commercial purposes in the late 1940s. Initially regarded as an exotic tool for squeezing a little extra profit out of existing wells, it gradually became a routine element of planning for new oil and natural gas wells. Since its post–World War II introduction, in fact, fracking has been used to stimulate production on an estimated 1 million natural gas and oil wells across the country.

Drilling and Casing the Well

The first step in the fracking process is drilling the well and casing it—placing a steel pipe down the hole. Once a gas company has identified a desirable drilling site and secured all legal rights and permits to engage in drilling operations, it uses seismic imaging technology to finalize a drilling plan. Seismic imaging involves bouncing sound waves off underground formations of shale and other types of rock. The unique sound wave signatures of various types of rock help well-site teams develop their subterranean route to the natural gas trapped beneath their feet.

In the meantime, workers clear and level 3 to 6 acres (1.2 to 2.4ha) of land surrounding the site. Some of this space is necessary to accommodate the large drilling equipment that is used. But the site—called a well pad—also requires a pit for the deposit of drilling waste and a storage area for the massive amounts of water that will be used. At some fracking well pads, as much as 10 million gallons (38 million L) of water may be used before a single fracking operation is complete.

An aerial view of a fracking operation in Tarrant County, Texas, in 2010.

Some wells are fracked a dozen times or more. In addition, well pads frequently contain two or more wells.

Once the property has been prepared, workers drill a well straight down through the earth to depths of anywhere from 6,000 feet (1,829m) to more than 14,000 feet (4,267m). The well depth is far deeper than the underground reservoirs of freshwater used for drinking; most residential wells are 100 to 150 feet (30m to 46m) deep, while commercial and municipal wells usually extend down no farther than 400 feet (122m). The drilled hole—called the bore hole or well bore—often passes near these water zones, however. That is why the length of the hole is outfitted with steel pipe known as surface casing. This metal sleeve, which is kept in place by concrete that is pumped into the space between the bore hole and the casing, is designed to shield those water resources from contamination from chemicals and water that will later be used in the fracking process. It also protects underground freshwater aquifers from the rock fragments and mud that are pushed up to the surface by the drill bits.

Up to this point, the drilling process for hydraulic fracturing operations aimed at extracting natural gas from shale rock formations is identical to that used for conventional oil and gas well operations. Once the concrete-enclosed steel casing is set, however, the processes diverge. Unlike conventional wells that feature vertically oriented bore holes, fracking wells veer off onto horizontal tracks to reach targeted shale formations. This is a vital distinction, according to John Duda, director of the National Energy Technology Laboratory's Strategic Center for Natural Gas and Oil. "It's important to note that hydraulic fracturing is different than drilling," he explained. "The drilling comes first and then the fracking."[13]

Key Steps in Horizontal Drilling

The shift to horizontal drilling begins when aboveground monitors indicate that the well bore has reached the shale formation that has been selected for fracking. This is known as the kickoff point or the heel. At the kickoff point, workers insert a Measurement While Drilling (MWD) motor into the bore hole. This device pushes the drill bit out of its vertical orientation onto a horizontal plane, known in the industry as a lateral. From there the drilling continues forward for another several thousand feet until the drill team at the surface finishes the shaft. In some operations this horizontal piping extends up to 1.4 miles (2.3km). The lateral is divided into a number of segments all the way to the end of the shaft, which is called the toe. Each of these segments is outfitted with metal casings.

Once the entire drilling process is complete—it can take anywhere from five to fourteen days—the drilling machinery is disassembled so that it can be transported to the next drilling site. As trucks haul the rig away, they leave behind a well that is ready to undergo the hydraulic fracturing process.

The Fracking Process, Step by Step

Fracking requires an arsenal of industrial equipment, including a slurry blender, high-pressure fracturing pumps, well-monitoring and chemical-additive devices, fracturing tanks, steel tubing, and trucks. The process begins with the delivery of powerful electrical charges into the far reaches of the well bore, all the way to the toe. These charges make punctures or perforations in the lateral casing, thus creating entry points to the surrounding shale formation.

FRACKING BRINGS BOOM TIMES

"Oh my heavens, yes, the [shale gas] boom is here. . . . The number of trucks on the roads is incredible, but the money is more than welcome here." —Ohio State University agricultural extension agent Mike Hogan, on hydraulic fracturing operations in eastern Ohio

Quoted in Dan Vergano. "Natural Gas Gold Rush: Is Your State Next?" *USA Today*, July 2, 2012. www.usatoday.com/news/nation/story/2012-05-29/fracking-environment -gas/55845708/1.

At this point the well is ready for the most important and well-known step in the fracking process—the injection of millions of gallons of highly pressurized liquid down into the well, using huge, diesel-powered hydraulic pumps. The liquid, or slickwater, is pushed into the entry points of the shale rock under such heavy force that it blasts open or fractures the shale. The natural gas previously trapped within the rock empties out through the newly created fissures into the well, where it can be easily extracted using conventional gas drilling technology.

The liquid used in fracking is composed mostly—but not entirely—of water. It is also lightly mixed with proppants and chemicals. Proppants are sand or ceramic materials that lodge in the cracks opened up by the high-pressure water and keep them propped open so that they cannot close again. The chemicals that are included in fracking liquid serve a variety of purposes. Some serve as lubricants to further increase the flow—and thus the power—of the injected water. This is where the term *slickwater* comes from. Other chemicals help dissolve rocks and sediments, eliminate unwanted bacteria in the water, control temperatures in the well bore, or protect the steel casing from

The Fracking Process

Hydraulic fracturing, or "fracking," involves the injection of more than a million gallons of water, sand and chemicals at high pressure down and across into horizontally drilled wells as far as 10,000 feet below the surface. The pressurized mixture causes the rock layer, in this case the Marcellus Shale, to crack. These fissures are held open by the sand particles so that natural gas from the shale can flow up the well.

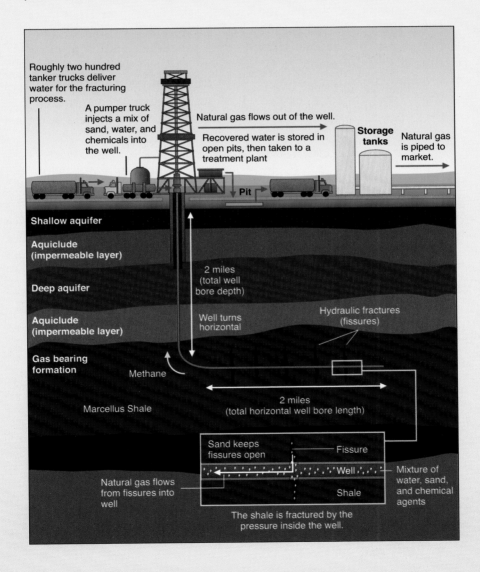

degradation. These chemicals usually account for less than 1 percent of the total volume of the injected slickwater, but some of them are highly toxic. Arguments over their impact on the environment and public health have made fracking chemicals the most controversial element of the entire hydraulic fracturing process.

Hydraulic fracturing proceeds on a section-by-section basis, beginning at the toe and working back horizontally to the heel. After each section is fracked, the work crew plugs it and moves on to the next section. This procedure requires multiple rounds of water to be pumped into the well bore. The fracking process transforms all of this liquid into "produced water" that contains the shale gas that has been freed from the rocks below. But the water also includes potentially dangerous chemicals.

The next step, then, is to separate the gas from this wastewater using high-tech evaporators and condensate tanks. This on-site treatment burns off the chemicals contained in the wastewater directly into the air. It also returns the natural gas to a vaporous state that allows it to be collected and piped to nearby compressor stations, where it undergoes further purification. It is then ready to be piped in gas form (or transported in liquid form) for use in electricity generation. According to Duda, "It's not that difficult to separate the water from the gas."[14]

Most of the wastewater produced during hydraulic fracturing remains deep underground, encased in the well's steel-and-concrete sheath. However, some of the wastewater—10 to 50 percent, depending on the operation—returns to the surface. This toxic mixture has to be carefully cleaned up and safely disposed of. The exact regulations for wastewater treatment and disposal vary from state to state. In some drilling operations, leftover wastewater is injected into deep disposal wells that lie hundreds or thousands of feet below freshwater aquifers. Other operators use trucks to take the wastewater to treatment plants. A third option employed by some fracking companies is to store the wastewater at the drilling site in big, open-air pits, where it gradually evaporates.

America's Historic Energy Heartland

The single largest shale formation in the United States that is being tapped for extraction of its natural gas resources is the Marcellus Shale, which extends in a broad arc from West Virginia all the way into New York State, passing through large swaths of Pennsylvania, Ohio, and Maryland along the way.

Of the five states that share the Marcellus Shale field, Pennsylvania and West Virginia in particular have been closely intertwined with the country's fossil fuel industries. Pennsylvania was the birthplace of the oil industry in the 1860s, and it remained the epicenter of U.S. oil exploration and refining operations for many decades thereafter. The economies of both states have also been heavily dependent on the coal industry for centuries, and coal mining and relat-

ed industries remain the single biggest economic force in West Virginia today.

Residents of Pennsylvania and West Virginia are thus more familiar with the benefits and drawbacks of fossil fuel–based economies than people in many other parts of the United States. They know firsthand how natural gas, coal, and oil development can provide economic growth and stability to families, neighborhoods, communities, and entire states. But oil and coal exploration and extraction activities have also wreaked lasting damage on some of the mountains, forests, rivers, and aquifers in their states. These instances of environmental degradation have complicated the efforts of shale gas companies to build public support for their Marcellus Shale operations.

Workers stand outside a West Virginia coal mine in 1908.

Site Remediation and Restoration

Most shale gas from hydraulic fracturing operations is captured in the first year, but industry scientists expect that many sites will deliver smaller but economically profitable levels of natural gas for decades to come. With this in mind, fracking wells often remain hooked up to larger natural gas pipeline networks long after the drilling crew has moved on to the next job.

Before withdrawing their machinery, trucks, and personnel from a site, however, companies that provide hydraulic fracturing services are responsible for restoring much of the land to its natural state. This process of site remediation and restoration is a strong area of emphasis for many companies. They recognize

A few pipes and tanks are all that remain on a former fracking site in Dimock, Pennsylvania. Drilling companies are responsible for restoring the sites used for their operations to their natural state.

Health Risks for Fracking Workers

Most of the headlines about the potential public health hazards associated with hydraulic fracturing focus on the health of people who live near fracking well sites. Increasingly, though, federal agencies have also expressed concerns about the possible health risks for workers at the site of fracking operations. In June 2012, for example, the Occupational Safety and Health Administration (OSHA) and the National Institute for Occupational Safety and Health (NIOSH) formally alerted members of the fracking industry about the danger posed to workers by silica exposure.

Sand used in hydraulic fracturing operations contains up to 99 percent silica. The danger is that the fracking process generates airborne dust containing high levels of silica. If workers inhale these silica-laden air particles, they run a greater risk of contracting the lung disease silicosis or developing other health problems associated with silica exposure.

According to NIOSH field studies at eleven fracking sites in five states, nearly 50 percent of workers at hydraulic fracturing sites had levels of silica exposure that exceeded OSHA's permissible limits, while nearly 80 percent of workers exceeded NIOSH's recommended limits.

that leaving acres of ruined-looking countryside behind damages the reputation of the entire industry. "The visual impacts of natural gas drilling are an important concern for residents and visitors of high-frequency drilling areas, both due to aesthetics and to impacts on property values and other industries, such as tourism,"[15] explained the authors of one study on fracking in the Marcellus Shale region.

According to the natural gas industry and fracking supporters, companies have become quite skilled at remediation. A 2012 pro-fracking article published in the *Economist*, for example, reported that at shale gas sites such as one operated by Chevron in southwestern Pennsylvania, observers can hardly tell that the site once housed a massive drilling rig and assorted heavy equipment and machinery. "After a little over a year of activity," asserted the *Economist*, "most of the land is reclaimed, apart from a little pipework and a water tank on a small section of the original site. . . . The only sound to disturb the replanted clover meadow is a faint whooshing as gas passes to an underground pipe network. It is the sound of dollars clocking up, and it could go on for 30–50 years."[16]

DISRUPTING RURAL AMERICA

"The area around the town of Silt, Colorado, used to be the kind of sleepy rural place where the tweet of birds was the most you would hear. Now it's hard to make out the birds because of the rumbling of natural gas drilling rigs. . . . Bare splotches of earth called well pads are all over the place." —National Public Radio reporter Elizabeth Shogren

Elizabeth Shogren. "'Close Encounters' with Gas Well Pollution." National Public Radio, May 15, 2012. www.npr.org/2012/05/15/149998263/close-encounters-with-gas-well-pollution.

Natural gas industry trade groups also encourage shale gas extraction companies to monitor all well sites regularly, even after the active fracking process has concluded. "Well tenders responsible for pad sites should be instructed to remain on the lookout for field conditions that may require immediate maintenance and repair," stated the Marcellus Shale Coalition, a Pennsylvania-based industry group.

> Vandals can breach site access controls and security measures at any time, and off-road vehicles can severely damage well pads, access roads and pipeline ROWs [rights-of-way], vegetation and drainage controls. Producers are encouraged to have well tenders and pipeline maintenance personnel remain vigilant. . . . Likewise, operators should encourage landowners with surface facilities on their properties to alert company personnel if any damage is observed.[17]

THE BENEFITS OF FRACKING

Many Americans support the use of fracking technology to obtain natural gas supplies that would otherwise remain tucked deep underground in shale rock formations. The most vocal and powerful advocates of hydraulic fracturing are the corporations that have a financial stake in the natural gas industry. They are by no means the only supporters of fracking, however. Many local, state, and federal government agencies and pro-business groups are supportive of the technology, as are many households and communities that see shale gas as a pathway to good jobs, economically vibrant downtowns, and lower utility bills.

Even some environmental activists and organizations have expressed support for fracking, as long as it takes place under regulations that protect air and water resources and public health. They believe that larger supplies of natural gas can reduce U.S. and world dependence on oil and coal, which generate greater volumes of air pollution and higher levels of greenhouse gases responsible for global warming.

Increased Energy Independence

One of the most frequently cited arguments in favor of fracking is that the additional natural gas it provides can greatly reduce American dependence on foreign energy sources. In 2009, for example, the U.S. Energy Information Administration reported that U.S. natural gas reserves grew by 30 percent once shale gas became extractable. That same year, the industry-funded Ground Water Protection Council estimated that shale gas and other unconventional natural gas resources had grown to account for 60 percent of the nation's total on-shore recoverable natural gas.

The jumps in natural gas reserves and natural gas consumption are a direct result of a tidal wave of new natural gas wells that use fracking technology. In 2011 a pro-fracking organization called the Institute for Energy Research proclaimed that "half of the gas consumed today [in the United States] was produced from wells drilled within the last 3.5 years."[18] The Energy Information Administration reported similar findings. It claimed that the new wells boosted U.S. natural gas production by 600 percent from 2006 to 2011.

A drilling rig marks the spot of a fracking operation in northern Pennsylvania in 2012.

These trends have been welcomed by Americans who say that developing additional domestic natural gas reserves can reduce U.S. imports of expensive oil from the Middle East, Venezuela, and other parts of the world, some of which have had historically troubled relations with the United States. Despite these encouraging figures, though, no one knows for sure how much once-unrecoverable natural gas can be extracted from underground shale basins through hydraulic fracturing.

Even the U.S. Department of Energy is unsure what lies beneath the nation's surface. In 2011, for instance, the agency estimated that about 827 trillion cubic feet (23.4 trillion cu. m) of natural gas could be recovered from shale deposits scattered across the United States. According to the Energy Department, about half of this recoverable gas—410 trillion cubic feet (11.6 trillion cu. m)—could be found in the Marcellus Shale alone. Only one year later, however, researchers at the Energy Department scaled back their estimates significantly. The agency's updated findings indicated that these shale formations contained only 482 trillion cubic feet (13.65 trillion cu. m) of recoverable natural gas. This marked a 42 percent decline from the previous year. Similarly, the agency cut its estimate of recoverable natural gas reserves in the Marcellus Shale formation by 66 percent, to 141 trillion cubic feet (4 trillion cu. m).

Why did these estimates change? Officials at the Energy Department explained that a lot of natural gas exploration and drilling occurred in the year between the two reports. The agency incorporated the findings from these efforts to update its estimates of U.S. gas reserves. But it also acknowledged that the 2012 estimates could be adjusted upward or further downward in the future, as additional gas exploration and extraction data become available.

Despite the uncertainty surrounding the exact amount of shale gas housed underground in the United States (and around the world), both supporters and critics of fracking agree that outlawing or severely restricting hydraulic fracturing would have a big impact on natural gas supplies. According to the industry group American Petroleum Institute, natural gas production in the United States would fall by 57 percent by 2018 if fracking were eliminated. Another industry group, the National Petroleum Council, claims that as many as four out of five of the nation's new natural gas wells require hydraulic fracturing processes to be productive. Armed with these types of figures, fracking advocates say that the practice has already become vital to America's quest for greater energy independence.

Good Jobs and Lower Living Expenses

The economic benefits associated with the development of shale gas reserves have also been highlighted by fracking supporters. Since the early 2000s about thirteen thousand new shale gas wells have been created on an annual basis—or about thirty-five a day. Thousands of these wells are located over the massive Marcellus Shale in the Northeast. According to a 2011 study by the pro-industry Manhattan Institute called *The Economic Opportunities of Shale Energy Development*, a single Marcellus well generates an average of sixty-two jobs and $5.46 million in economic output.

COMMUNITY ADJUSTMENTS TO FRACKING

"Too often 'fracking' gets blamed when it's the whole package that leads to the problems—the trucks, the noise, the workers, the environmental problems, the feeling of being disempowered by regulations." —Pennsylvania State University sociologist Kathy Brasier

Quoted in Dan Vergano. "Natural Gas Gold Rush: Is Your State Next?" *USA Today*, July 2, 2012. www.usatoday.com/news/nation/story/2012-05-29/fracking-environment-gas/55845708/1.

This output covers employment and economic activity directly related to pad preparation, drilling, fracking, and other aspects of well development and maintenance. It also includes businesses that provide goods and services to the natural gas industry—"everything from selling workers donuts to making steel pipes used in the process. One-time lease checks [to property owners]—some for more than six figures—also can juice local economies,"[19] noted *USA Today*. "It's unbelievable,

A worker climbs the stairs of a drilling rig at a natural gas well in Medicine Lodge, Kansas. The jobs created by fracking operations have been described as having a "transformative" effect on local and state economies.

the opportunity," said Frank Puskarich, a Pennsylvania business owner who has greatly expanded his mobile barbeque business to feed gas industry workers. "And it's not just me. It's leather makers, grocery stores, truck drivers, guys with dump trucks."[20]

In addition to hefty cash payments, landowners sometimes receive additional financial compensation for use of their land in the form of royalties. Royalties are a modest percentage of the overall income generated by the well or wells on their property. These infusions of cash can be extremely helpful to farmers who own large plots of rural land, where fracking operations are concentrated. Many American farmers struggle financially under the weight of events they cannot control, from droughts and flooding to general economic downturns. "For those people," explained writer Seamus McGraw, "the promise of a few hundred dollars an acre up front, with the possibility of far greater riches—perhaps millions of dollars—down the road, was a godsend."[21]

The fracking industry's ability to generate jobs, though, remains an even bigger selling point. "It comes down to employment," said Daniel Yergin in a 2011 interview. "Shale gas has created hundreds and hundreds and hundreds of thousands of jobs in the last five years in the United States. It's brought $1 billion of revenue into the state government of Pennsylvania [where development of Marcellus Shale has been most intensive]. . . . It does have a transformative impact."[22] The natural gas companies that are members of America's Natural Gas Alliance, a trade group, agreed. In 2012 the group released a study that claimed fracking and other unconventional natural gas activities employed 1 million Americans in 2010 and that employment in the unconventional gas field could jump to more than 2.4 million by 2035.

Jobs have emerged as a major consideration in places that have yet to decide whether to allow fracking to take place. The state of New York, for example, is considering whether to lift a moratorium—a legal suspension—of fracking operations within its borders, which includes significant stretches of the Marcellus Shale field. Supporters of natural gas exploration in the state constantly emphasize the possible job benefits of doing so. Ending the moratorium would create fifteen thousand to eighteen thousand jobs in southwestern New York, according to the Manhattan Institute, and as many as ninety thousand additional jobs in eastern New York.

Fracking advocates also emphasize that increased business activity and new jobs bring additional tax revenues to communities and states. This money can be used to build and repair roads and bridges, construct new schools and improve existing ones, purchase new fire trucks and street lights, and develop and maintain softball fields, bike trails, parks, and other recreational facilities.

A FORCE FOR GOOD

"A responsible mix of regulation, transparency, liability and corporate-community exchanges can produce economic and energy benefits while limiting environmental risks." —Andrew C. Revkin, environmental journalist and blogger for *Dot Earth*, an environmental blog at the *New York Times*

Andrew C. Revkin. "Next Steps on Gas Fracking in New York." *Dot Earth* (blog), *New York Times*, January 23, 2012. http://dotearth.blogs.nytimes.com/2012/01/23/next -steps-on-gas-fracking-in-new-york.

Finally, supporters note that as the supply of natural gas increases, its cost to consumers goes down. According to some estimates, fracking helped cut gas prices by 25 percent from 2008 to the beginning of 2012. This price decline has made it easier for American households to pay for their energy use. It also leaves them with more income to spend on other goods and services, which benefits the economy as a whole. "The economic benefits of shale gas drilling far outweigh the environmental costs,"[23] summarized the Manhattan Institute study.

Exaggerated Environmental Fears

The natural gas industry and other supporters of hydraulic fracturing recognize that doubts about the environmental and public health safety of fracking stand as the single biggest obstacle to the practice. Fracking enthusiasts worry that these fears could prevent New York and some other states from approving shale gas operations. They also express concern that lawmakers might impose regulations on the industry that will keep it from reaching its full economic potential.

Fracking advocates have addressed these perceived threats by reassuring the public that hydraulic fracturing is safe for the environment. According to them, fracking fears stem in large part from misinformation spread by "environmental extremists" like Josh Fox, a documentary filmmaker who released the anti-fracking movie *Gasland* in 2010, and "alarmists" like Ian Urbina, who published a hard-hitting series of articles on fracking in the *New York Times*. Supporters of fracking insist that Fox, Urbina, and other critics greatly exaggerate the industry's impact on air quality, drinking water, and ecosystems.

The environmental issue that crops up most often in conjunction with fracking is water contamination. Critics have charged, for example, that some rivers and lakes suffer ecological damage when hydraulic fracturing operations dump waste-water in them. They also assert that the water treatment plants

Signs warning of the dangers of fracking are posted in a yard in Evans City, Pennsylvania. Proponents of shale gas drilling face strong opposition from those who are convinced the practice is a danger to the environment and public health.

that treat fracking wastewater in many states are not equipped to remove all the toxic chemicals and radiation it contains before they release the water into area rivers and other waterways (when fracking wastewater returns to the surface, it sometimes contains radioactive minerals from the shale).

Defenders of fracking admit that some states could do more to protect their rivers. But they say that most shale gas companies are recycling ever-higher percentages of their wastewater or safely disposing of it underground. The natural gas industry and its allies also insist that states with a lot of fracking activity, like Texas and Pennsylvania, have established wastewater treatment procedures that provide good protection to river ecosystems and the drinking water those rivers provide. "There is no doubt that drilling wastewater is highly polluted," said John Hanger, who served as secretary of Pennsylvania's Department of Environmental Protection until early 2011. "Prior to the Marcellus, when the Pennsylvania industry was small, we were dumping drilling wastewater untreated into rivers and streams and hoping that dilution would keep concentrations below levels that would cause damage to aquatic life or drinking water." Hanger indicated, though, that Pennsylvania and most other states have learned their lesson: "There is probably less water going untreated into the rivers today than before the first Marcellus well. It's a success story. If you look at the top ten things impacting water in Pennsylvania right now, the gas industry would not be on the list, and certainly not fracking. Industry, environmentalists, and regulators all ought to be celebrating."[24]

Protecting Underground Water Supplies

Energy companies involved in hydraulic fracturing have also rejected claims that the toxic chemicals contained in fracking slickwater have contaminated some underground aquifers used for drinking water. As the industry website EnergyFromShale.org stated:

> In addition to Federal rules, statutes and regulations have been implemented in every oil and natural gas producing state to ensure that operations are conducted in an environmentally responsible fashion. All state drilling

regulations specifically address groundwater protection, including requirements for the surface casing to be set below the lowest groundwater aquifer. This casing in combination with other steel casing and cement sheaths that are subsequently installed protects the groundwater with multiple layers of protection for the life of the well. Additional protection is offered by the impermeable rock formations that lie between the oil and natural gas formations and the groundwater, formations that have isolated the groundwater over millions of years.[25]

The industry and state and federal regulators have acknowledged isolated cases where faulty well construction has contaminated local groundwater supplies with toxic chemicals or methane, which is the main component of natural gas. The natural gas industry has consistently stated, however, that these cases simply show the need to make sure that wells—whether built for conventional drilling or fracking—are properly constructed and sealed. Industry trade groups have pledged that as fracking moves forward, all wells will be carefully built and monitored to make them as safe as possible.

For most of the life of the fracking industry, regulators, scientists, and journalists have echoed industry claims that fracking does not threaten groundwater supplies. "The idea stressed by fracking critics that deep-injected fluids will migrate into groundwater is mostly false," wrote McGraw in a 2011 issue of *Popular Mechanics*. "A fracture caused by the drilling process would have to extend through the several thousand feet of rock that separate deep shale gas deposits from freshwater aquifers. . . . It would be like stacking a dozen bricks on top of each other . . . and expecting a crack in the bottom brick to extend all the way to the top one."[26] *New York Times* environmental reporter and blogger Andrew C. Revkin agreed. In 2012 he wrote, "There are clearly problems with well integrity and methane migration . . . [but] the evidence of large-scale aquifer contamination simply is not there."[27]

In late 2011 and 2012, however, a flurry of news stories raised fresh doubts about the impact of fracking operations on water quality in underground aquifers and nearby rivers and

Fracking and the Case of the Flaming Faucet

One of the best-known scenes in the anti-fracking documentary *Gasland*, directed by Josh Fox, shows a Colorado resident turning on his kitchen faucet and holding a flame to the water. A fireball erupts out of the water, an event that the filmmaker attributes to well contamination from fracking. According to an investigation carried out by the Colorado Oil and Gas Conservation Commission (COGCC), however, the homeowner's water troubles were not due to fracking. Instead, the agency determined that his well had been drilled accidently into a naturally occurring bed of "biogenic" methane gas close to the surface. Fox criticized the COGCC's findings, arguing that the agency still failed to "identify the migratory pathway of the gas" into the homeowner's water supply. "Just because [the homeowner's] gas is 'biogenic' doesn't mean that its migration into wa-

ter supplies was not caused by drilling," he added.

The COGCC report did indicate that another nearby homeowner's water *was* contaminated as a result of a flawed fracking operation. The agency acknowledged that this kind of contamination can occur when the drilling hole is not properly sealed. Other state agencies have adopted the same basic position as the COGCC. They reject claims that fracking endangers major underground aquifers, but they acknowledge that in individual cases, sloppy fracking activity has contaminated home wells. In May 2011, for example, the state of Pennsylvania fined Chesapeake Energy $1 million for contaminating the water supplies of sixteen families.

Josh Fox. "Affirming *Gasland*." *Gasland*: A Film by Josh Fox, July 2010, p. 8. http://1trickpony.cachefly.net /gas/pdf/Affirming_Gasland_Sept_2010.pdf.

Water from a well contaminated with methane catches fire as it pours from the faucet.

streams. In December 2011 the U.S. Environmental Protection Agency (EPA) released a study indicating that groundwater supplies around the small town of Pavilion, Wyoming, had likely been *directly* contaminated by seepage from a shale formation that had undergone fracking. Three months later the *New York Times* reported that secret documents from the EPA, state regulators, and hydraulic fracturing companies all indicated that

> [fracking] wastewater, which is sometimes hauled to sewage plants not designed to treat it and then discharged into rivers that supply drinking water, contains radioactivity at levels higher than previously known, and far higher than the level that federal regulators say is safe for these treatment plants to handle. . . . Most of these facilities cannot remove enough of the radioactive material to meet federal drinking-water standards before discharging the wastewater into rivers, sometimes just miles upstream from drinking-water intake plants.[28]

Environmental and public health groups said that these reports were made even more troubling by the fact that water treatment plants in Pennsylvania and many other states almost never test for radiation in their water.

Gas companies that have been implicated in these reports have strongly defended their fracking record. In the Pavilion case, for example, the company responsible for the alleged aquifer contamination claimed that the EPA study was deeply flawed and that the agency's "conclusions do not stand up to the rigor of a non-partisan, scientific-based review."[29] Other industry defenders claim that the Wyoming findings are unique because the fracking wells in Pavilion were much shallower—and thus much closer to water resources—than fracking sites in most other parts of the country.

Fracking supporters also insist that the threat of poisoning of water supplies from radiation and fracking fluid has been greatly exaggerated. They emphasize that in Pennsylvania, officials carried out a series of radiation tests on state drinking water in response to the *New York Times* article. In 2012 the officials reported that they found nondetectable or minor levels of

A worker at a treatment plant unloads wastewater hauled away from a fracking site. The proper handling of wastewater is considered a key aspect of minimizing the environmental impact of shale gas drilling.

radiation that posed no threat to public safety. That same year, gas companies and their defenders seized on an Associated Press story that rejected "fracktivist" claims of a linkage between fracking activity and higher breast cancer rates. "Researchers checked [Texas] state health data and found no evidence of an increase in [breast cancer in] the counties where the spike supposedly occurred,"[30] reported Kevin Begos of the Associated Press. For their part, fracking opponents like Fox claimed that Begos's article was biased against environmentalists and misrepresented scientific data. "It's fine for him to have an opinion about whether or not gas drilling causes health problems," wrote Fox. "But it is not fine to cherry pick data and present only one side of the story while claiming to be an impartial journalist."[31]

Media Perceptions of Fracking

In February 2012 the Energy Institute at the University of Texas–Austin released a comprehensive study of environmental regulations governing the practice of hydraulic fracturing for shale gas development. As part of their examination, the researchers conducted a study of media coverage of fracking in three major shale gas areas—the six-state Marcellus Shale region, Louisiana's Haynesville Shale region, and Texas's Barnett Shale region.

According to the Energy Institute analysis of news coverage (including national and local newspapers, television, radio, and online sources), the majority of news stories on fracking were negative in tone. These findings extended to local news coverage—79 percent of newspaper stories and 70 percent of television stories on the Barnett Shale, for example, were negative in tone. But they were also evident at the national level, as the table below shows.

Opponents of fracking say that these results show that the practice has numerous environmental and safety problems. Supporters of fracking, on the other hand, believe that the study shows that news coverage has been unfairly slanted against hydraulic fracturing.

Charles G. Groat and Thomas W. Grimshaw. *Fact-Based Regulation for Environmental Protection in Shale Gas Development.* Energy Institute, University of Texas–Austin, February 2012, p. 12. http://energy.utexas.edu/images/ei_shale_gas_reg_summary1202.pdf.

	Negative	Neutral	Positive
National newspapers (3)	64%	25%	12%
Metropolitan newspapers (10)	65%	23%	12%
National television & radio (7)	64%	19%	18%
Metropolitan television (18)	70%	27%	3%
Online news (1)	63%	30%	7%

Sustainable Consumption of Freshwater

The fracking industry has also tried to reassure public concerns about the amount of water used in its operations. This task is easier in the water-rich Marcellus Shale states of New York, Pennsylvania, Ohio, and West Virginia. *Popular Mechanics* reported in 2011, for example, that a study by Carnegie Mellon University found that "the amount of water required to drill all 2,916 of the Marcellus wells permitted in Pennsylvania in the first 11 months of 2010 would equal the amount of drinking water used by just one city, Pittsburgh, during the same period."[32] Another scholar at Penn State's Marcellus Center for Outreach and Research reported that while natural gas development activities in Pennsylvania use 1.9 million gallons (7.2 million L) a day, other state industries like mining (96 million gallons, or 363.4 million L, a day) and agricultural livestock (62 million gallons, or 234.7 million L, a day) use much more water.

The natural gas industry acknowledges that the situation is different in arid and semiarid regions of the United States. In these places, limited water supplies have to be shared by a wide range of users. But energy companies and other supporters of fracking say that is it unfair to single out their industry's water use, especially since hydraulic fracturing is economically beneficial in other ways.

In Colorado, for example, where the industry has experienced enormous growth in recent years due to fracking, the Colorado Oil and Gas Association estimated that fracking operations would use 6.5 trillion gallons in 2012. This amount, they emphasized, was just over one-tenth of 1 percent of total water use in the state. Gas companies and state officials in Colorado and other regions of the West also claim that water conservation is an important factor in all of their new fracking projects.

A Tool in the Fight Against Global Warming

One environmental issue that fracking supporters are eager to talk about is global climate change, also known as global warming. They say that hydraulic fracturing's capacity to capture natural gas is making the United States and the rest of the world less dependent on coal, which burns dirtier—emits greater volumes of air pollutants and greenhouse gases that cause global warming—than any other energy source. Many environmental organizations agreed with this assessment when fracking came on the scene. Some of them even described natural gas obtained from fracking as a major new weapon in the fight against global climate change, along with so-called renewable energy sources like solar and wind power. Both

A flare burns atop a natural gas well awaiting connection to a pipeline in Bradford County, Pennsylvania. Advocates point to natural gas as the key to reducing the consumption of coal and oil, which emit pollutants linked to global climate change.

the Republican administration of President George W. Bush (2001–2009) and the Democratic administration of President Barack Obama (2009–) have also described shale gas as a valuable resource that can reduce consumption of oil and gasoline, both of which are leading drivers of global warming.

The impact of rising natural gas supplies was quickly felt in the coal industry. From 2009 to 2012 coal's share of America's total power production fell from half to about one-third, as utility companies switched from coal (and oil) to less-expensive gas. During this same period, though, many environmental activists reconsidered their belief that shale gas could help combat global warming. This change of heart stemmed from a flurry of studies indicating that the cumulative impact of fracking—including its reliance on emissions-spewing trucks and its inability to keep significant amounts of methane from escaping into the atmosphere—made it a significant contributor to global warming in its own right.

The energy industry and its supporters, though, have little patience for this reversal. "No industrial process is completely benign, and all have environmental consequences," wrote Ronald Bailey, science editor for *Reason* magazine.

The relevant question is: Do the benefits outweigh the costs? Are people better off using the resource than they would otherwise be? Of course, any company that damages someone else's property should be fully liable for the costs. But if you're worried about man-made global warming, natural gas remains the affordable way to supply lower-carbon energy to the world as technologists work to bring renewable energy costs down.[33]

CHAPTER 4

THE DRAWBACKS
OF FRACKING

In the few years since hydraulic fracturing emerged as a major tool of the natural gas industry, complaints about its negative effects on the environment and public health have steadily increased in number and intensity. Critics of fracking charge that it is contaminating local water supplies, degrading the environmental health of sensitive wilderness areas, tearing apart rural communities, contributing to global warming, and endangering the health of thousands of families who live near fracking sites.

A Threat to Groundwater Aquifers?

The most high-profile controversy surrounding shale gas production centers on its impact on nearby rivers, streams, and underground aquifers. The natural gas industry admits that hydraulic fracturing operations have contaminated drinking water supplies in isolated instances. Fracking advocates claim that this problem has been exaggerated, though, and that it can be solved through better sealing of gas wells. Opponents say that the problem is much more severe than the industry admits. "There is no such thing as a leakproof gas well," wrote anti-fracking activists Josh Fox and Barbara Arrindell.

> Industry reports on the problem point to its persistence and the impossibility of completely preventing it. . . . Leaking oil and gas wells are more than statistics. Failure rates mean thousands across the nation have enough contaminants in their water and land to render them unfit for residential or agricultural use. They're left with homes they are forced to abandon, and compromised health.[34]

According to the investigative journalism organization Pro-Publica, the problem of leaking wells is a significant one. A Pro-Publica review of two hundred thousand inspections of fracking wells and wastewater disposal wells across America from late 2007 to late 2010 found seventeen thousand violations—one for every six wells. More than seven thousand of the wells showed signs of leakage. "Most well failures are patched within six months of being discovered, EPA data shows, but with as much as five years passing between integrity tests, it can take a while for leaks to be discovered," noted ProPublica. "And not every well can be repaired. Kansas shut down at least 47 injection wells in 2010. . . . Louisiana shut down 82. Wyoming shut down 144."[35] In addition, environmentalists and public health advocates claim that underground water supplies have been poisoned by spills and leaks from aboveground pits that hold fracking wastewater.

A jug contains fouled drinking water from the faucet of a home in Dimock, Pennsylvania, where residents allege their wells were contaminated by fracking operations beginning in 2008.

Most early reports of groundwater contamination from fracking were concentrated in the West, where the practice first became established. In Colorado, for example, forty-eight cases of suspected water contamination from oil and gas wells were reported in 2008 alone. That same year, toxic fluid seeped into water supplies at more than eight hundred oil and gas drilling sites in New Mexico. People in Western communities also began complaining that nearby fracking activity had turned their drinking water black, given it a metallic taste, or even made it flammable, as demonstrated in Fox's documentary *Gasland*. More recently, however, the shale gas boom has shifted to northern Appalachia, a mountainous region of the northeastern United States stretching from New York State down through Pennsylvania and Ohio into West Virginia. It is here that the most heavily publicized stories of groundwater contamination have been concentrated.

A FUTURE OF POLLUTED WATER?

"In 10 to 100 years we are going to find out that most of our groundwater is polluted. A lot of people are going to get sick, and a lot of people may die." —Former EPA fracking expert Mario Salazar

Quoted in Abrahm Lustgarten and ProPublica. "Are Fracking Wastewater Wells Poisoning the Ground Beneath Our Feet?" *Scientific American*, June 21, 2012. www .scientificamerican.com/article.cfm?id=are-fracking-wastewater-wells-poisoning -ground-beneath-our-feeth.

Since 2008 the U.S. fracking industry has been centered in Pennsylvania in particular. A good portion of the massive gas-saturated Marcellus Shale formation lies directly under the state. Unlike the state of New York, which has imposed a moratorium on fracking, most Pennsylvania lawmakers and officials have greeted the natural gas industry with open arms. Landowners in Pennsylvania initially welcomed fracking operations on their lands as well. Environmental organizations, public health advocates, and grassroots citizens' groups now say, though, that many rural Pennsylvanians have come to regret their decision to lease their land to frackers.

The most famous backlash against hydraulic fracturing came from Dimock, a small town in northeastern Pennsylvania. "Dimock is now known as the place where . . . people's water started turning brown and making them sick, one woman's water well spontaneously combusted, and horses and pets mysteriously began to lose their hair,"[36] wrote journalist Christopher Bateman. Fracking critics note that all of these problems erupted only after 2008, when the Cabot Oil and Gas Corporation initiated extensive hydraulic fracturing operations around the township.

The dispute between Cabot and residents worsened with each passing month, fed by fresh reports of mysterious illnesses, foul well water, and allegations that Cabot was trying to intimidate and spy on its opponents. The battle lines further hardened when state environmental regulators determined that Cabot had indeed polluted Dimock's groundwater supply. In early 2012 an EPA study concluded that Dimock's water was safe to drink, but this judgment failed to reassure Dimock residents, public health experts, and environmental groups. "What the agency didn't say—at least, not publicly— is that the water samples contained dangerous quantities of methane gas, a finding that confirmed some of the agency's initial concerns and the complaints raised by Dimock residents since 2009," reported ProPublica.

> The test results also showed the group of wells contained dozens of other contaminants, including low levels of chemicals known to cause cancer and heavy metals that exceed the agency's "trigger level" and could lead to illness if consumed over an extended period of time. The EPA's assurances suggest that the substances detected do not violate specific drinking water standards, but no such standards exist for some of the contaminants and some experts said the agency should have acknowledged that they were detected at all.[37]

In August 2012 the bitter legal clash between Cabot and Dimock residents finally came to a close when the two sides reached a confidential financial settlement.

Lifting the Veil of Secrecy
over Fracking Chemicals

Critics of fracking say that a great deal of the fear surrounding potential contamination of drinking water is due to the fact that the public does not know precisely which chemicals are used in the process. By the time that fracking became extensive enough to capture the attention of regulators, policy makers, and the public, the so-called Halliburton Loophole of 2005 had granted the gas industry the right to keep its fracking formulas secret. From that point on, the EPA and state-level health and environmental agencies had no way of tracking the public's exposure to those chemicals. If these agencies do not know what chemicals are being used, they cannot monitor their use or the extent to which they are migrating into water supplies. "We don't have a great handle on the toxicology of fracking chemicals,"[38] admitted Vikas Kapil, chief medical officer at the National Center for Environmental Health, which is one of the Centers for Disease Control and Prevention.

Despite these disadvantages, journalists, environmental researchers, and scientists (most notably Theo Colborn) have, over the course of several years, managed to identify some of the chemicals commonly used to create fracking fluid. These include benzene, ethylbenzene, toluene, xylene, and other chemicals that are either known carcinogens—cancer-causing agents—or toxic to humans and aquatic species.

In mid-2011 a special congressional report on fracking commissioned by Democratic members of the House Committee on Energy and Commerce found that between 2005 and 2009, the fourteen leading hydraulic fracturing companies in the United States used over 2,500 hydraulic fracturing products. Approximately 650 of these products included at least one of twenty-nine chemicals that are known or suspected human carcinogens, regulated under the Safe Drinking Water Act, or listed as hazardous air pollutants. Such findings led the report's authors to conclude, "Companies are injecting fluids containing unknown chemicals about which they may have limited understanding of the potential risks posed to human health and the environment."[39]

Methane	
Methane	12/9/2010
Methane	10/22/2010
Methane	1/20/2010
Methane	10/22/2010
Methane	12/03/10
Methane	12/09/10
Nickel	8/12/2010
Nickel	1/20/2010
Nitrate	1/21/2010
Nitrate	9/24/2010
Nitrate	11/19/2010
Nitrate	9/24/2010
Nitrite	

A Pennsylvania resident reviews the results of a test for contaminants in a sample of drinking water in 2012. Less than half of the states where shale gas is drilled require companies to publicly disclose the chemicals used in their operations.

Since 2010 the mystery surrounding the fracking fluids used by the gas industry has been partially lifted in some parts of the country. Seven states—Arkansas, Colorado, Montana, Ohio, Pennsylvania, Texas, and Wyoming—have passed laws requiring fracking companies to publicly disclose the chemicals they use. In July 2012, however, the Natural Resources Defense Council (NRDC) released a study that found that only two of those states—Montana and Wyoming—mandated disclosure of the *amount* of fracking chemicals used. Further, the NRDC found that of at least twenty-nine states with fracking operations within their borders, only fourteen had public disclosure requirements of any kind. In addition, the NRDC asserted, "every state that does have rules fails to require disclosure of many important aspects of fracking; most states with rules allow companies to exploit 'trade secret' exemptions to prevent disclosure of any information the company decides is confidential; [and] enforcement is spotty, so the disclosure requirements that do exist are sometimes ignored."[40]

Urging Americans to Look Beyond Fossil Fuels

During her career as an environmental journalist and writer, Elizabeth Kolbert has documented the many ways in which heavy U.S. reliance on fossil fuels, or hydrocarbons, has damaged the environment. She views the rise of fracking skeptically, as the following excerpt from a 2011 commentary published in *New Yorker* magazine makes clear:

> Americans have never met a hydrocarbon they didn't like. Oil, natural gas, liquefied natural gas, tar-sands oil, coal-bed methane, and coal, which is, mostly, carbon—the country loves them all, not wisely, but too well. To the extent that the United States has an energy policy, it is perhaps best summed up as: if you've got it, burn it. . . .
>
> In the end, the best case to be made for fracking is that much of what is already being done is probably even worse. The trouble with this sort of argument is that, in the absence of a rational energy policy, there's no reason to substitute shale gas for coal. We can combust them both! The way things now stand, there's nothing to prevent us from getting wasted mountains *and* polluted drinking water, and a ruined climate to boot.
>
> In the coming decades, ever-improving technologies will almost certainly make new sources of hydrocarbons accessible. At some point, either we will outgrow our infatuation or we will burn our way to a very dark place.

Elizabeth Kolbert. "Burning Love." *New Yorker*, December 5, 2011. www.newyorker.com/talk/comment/2011/12/05/111205taco_talk_kolbert.

Concerns About Rivers, Forests, and Wildlife

The NRDC and other conservation groups also say that fracking pollutes and desecrates rivers, streams, and forests that are part of America's natural heritage and provide important habitat for wildlife. They claim that inadequate regulations and poor enforcement of existing environmental rules have allowed drilling companies to damage—and in some cases ruin—these resources without any meaningful punishment. For example, rampant gas development in previously undeveloped wilderness areas has been blamed for downturns in populations of some wildlife species in Wyoming and Colorado.

Fracking opponents also point to waterways like Dunkard Creek, a once healthy and attractive stream along the Pennsylvania–West Virginia border. Opponents of hydraulic fracturing believe that more than 30 miles (48km) of the stream was thoroughly poisoned in the fall of 2009 by illegal dumping of fracking wastewater. Critics have also complained about contamination of larger waterways like Pennsylvania's Monongahela River. Water quality declined so rapidly in that river after the onset of the fracking boom that in 2009 state authorities issued a temporary warning to 325,000 residents who get drinking water from the Monongahela to avoid drinking tap water from their homes.

Environmental groups and public health experts note that contamination of rivers and streams from fracking wastewater has occurred both from illegal dumping and from accidental spills

A member of a conservation group reaches into a Pennsylvania creek in June 2011 for a water sample to be tested for contaminants linked to fracking operations in the area.

from storage pits. According to them, however, the bigger problem lies with the industry's usage of sewage treatment facilities to "clean" the toxin-laced wastewater the operations generate. Fracking companies haul their wastewater to these plants, which are supposed to scrub it free of pollutants and then discharge it into area rivers. In the northeastern United States, for example, major river basins like the Ohio, Monongahela, and Susquehanna that collectively supply drinking water to tens of millions of Americans have all received gas-drilling wastewater. Scientific studies and investigative reports from federal and state agencies have revealed, however, that many water treatment plants are unable to remove certain toxins and contaminants used in fracking.

Bringing Dangerous Radioactive Materials to the Surface

Public health advocates and environmental activists also warn that fracking wastewater may contain potentially dangerous radioactive materials. These naturally occurring radioactive elements are usually safely locked away deep underground, but fracking can sometimes dislodge them and bring them to the surface within the wastewater generated by the procedure.

In 2011 a *New York Times* investigation helmed by environmental reporter Ian Urbina found that at least twelve sewage treatment plants in three states had discharged wastewater that was only partly treated into rivers, lakes, and streams over the previous three years. Urbina reported:

> Of more than 179 wells producing wastewater with high levels of radiation, at least 116 reported levels of radium or other radioactive materials 100 times as high as the levels set by federal drinking-water standards. At least 15 wells produced wastewater carrying more than 1,000 times the amount of radioactive elements considered acceptable. The . . . danger of radioactive wastewater is its potential to contaminate drinking water or enter the food chain through fish or farming. Once radium enters a person's body, by eating, drinking, or breathing, it can cause cancer and other health problems.[41]

Treated wastewater flows into the Niagara River in Niagara Falls, New York, in February 2012, a month before the city's leaders voted to ban their municipal plant from handling wastewater from fracking operations, citing public health concerns.

Despite this fact, wrote Urbina, many facilities that draw from rivers, lakes, and streams for drinking water are only rarely required to test for radiation in the water they release into communities. In 2011, for example, the *New York Times* reported that it had "reviewed data from more than 65 intake plants downstream from some of the busiest drilling regions in the state [of Pennsylvania]. No one has tested for radioactivity since 2008, and most have not tested since at least 2005, before most of the drilling waste was being produced."[42]

These kinds of reports have led a broad array of environmental organizations and public health groups to call for either moratoriums on fracking or sweeping new industry regulations to better protect the environment and public health. The river conservation group American Rivers, for example, declared in 2012:

In the push to develop domestic sources of energy nationwide, the direct and cumulative impacts to water quality in streams and rivers have been largely ignored and accountability for environmental degradation has been lax at best. Unchecked by adequate safeguards, natural gas production has the potential to pollute clean water for millions of people. We have already experienced instances of surface and groundwater pollution, air pollution, soil contamination, habitat fragmentation, and erosion from extracting gas from shale using fracking where proper safeguards were not in place or followed.[43]

Fracking and Sustainable Water Use

Most of the water-themed headlines surrounding fracking have focused on whether it poses a contamination threat to groundwater aquifers and ecologically sensitive rivers and other waterways. Some environmental groups and urban planning experts, however, have also cautioned that heavy consumption of water by shale gas operations could contribute to water shortages, es-

A tanker truck is filled with fresh water to bring to a shale gas drilling site in Pennsylvania. Many environmentalists are critical of the large amount of water consumed by fracking operations.

pecially in arid and semiarid regions of the western United States. They describe the issue as one of simple arithmetic. It takes from 1 million to 7 million gallons (3.8 million L to 26.5 million L) of water to frack a well, and a single well may be fracked a dozen or more times. This procedure has already been done to hundreds of thousands of wells, and industry and government analysts expect the annual arrival of twenty thousand to thirty thousand new fracking wells over the next several years. In 2010 the EPA estimated that 70 billion to 140 billion gallons (265 billion L to 530 billion L) of water are used for hydraulic fracturing operations in the United States each year.

A MOTHER'S WARNING

"[Fracking] is ruining us. I'm not an activist, an alarmist, a Democrat, environmentalist, or anything like that. I'm just a person who isn't able to manage the health of my family because of all this drilling." — Kelly Gant, a resident of Bartonville, Texas, whose daughter and son have experienced severe asthma attacks, headaches, and other health problems since a fracking well was installed near their home

Quoted in Ian Urbina. "Regulation Lax as Gas Wells' Tainted Water Hits Rivers." *New York Times*, February 26, 2011. www.nytimes.com/2011/02/27/us/27gas.html ?pagewanted=all.

Some observers believe that these trends could create some serious problems in the not-too-distant future. They speculate that fracking could contribute to municipal shortages of drinking water and to damaging withdrawals of water from rivers, lakes, and reservoirs that are valued both for recreation and as wildlife habitat. In Colorado, for example, environmental advocate Gary Wockner wrote, "Many fast-growing . . . cities predict they will have a shortage of water in the next decade and are already proposing new water supply projects that will further drain Colorado's already severely degraded rivers. And, the very same cities that are proposing new water projects are also selling increasing amounts of water for fracking."[44]

Wockner acknowledges that estimates of the fracking industry's water needs vary considerably. As he wrote:

> The industry-funded Colorado Oil and Gas Association estimates that water used for fracking could be 20,000 acre feet (6.5 billion gallons) per year . . . but some environmentalists believe that number would be higher as tens-of-thousands of new wells are drilled and fracked, as old wells are re-fracked, and as that water is never returned to the hydrologic cycle because it is too poisoned and polluted for other uses.[45]

Either way, observers like Wockner believe that Colorado and other states already straining under existing water demands need to pay more attention to the industry's escalating water consumption. Wockner wrote:

> Fracking may only need a small percentage of [Colorado's total water]. But more importantly and to the point, it is also true that fracking is a brand new use of water, and that the brand new amount of water needed for fracking is coming from many of the same cities that are proposing brand new water projects that will further dam, drain, and divert the last streamflows out of Colorado's rivers.[46]

Concerns About Air Pollution

Public health researchers and environmental organizations have also issued numerous warnings about the impact of fracking on air quality. They claim that studies indicate a clear linkage between emissions from hydraulic fracturing operations and elevated levels of air pollution and associated health problems—especially for people who live near well sites.

In Fort Worth, Texas, chemical emissions from natural gas operations in and around the city had by 2010 grown to the point that they matched the city's total emissions from cars and trucks. The state of Wyoming, meanwhile, "no longer meets federal air quality standards because of fumes seeping from the state's 27,000 wells,"[47] wrote environmentalist Bill McKibben. In Wyoming's Sublette County, for example, the land is so light-

The Public Health Danger Posed by Methane

According to Abrahm Lustgarten of the nonprofit investigative journalism organization ProPublica, many Americans have only a vague understanding of the public health dangers associated with methane. After all, Lustgarten acknowledged, "drinking water with methane, the largest component of natural gas, isn't necessarily harmful. The gas itself isn't toxic—the Environmental Protection Agency doesn't even regulate it—and it escapes from water quickly, like bubbles in a soda."

Lustgarten added, though, that methane can become life-threatening in certain situations. "The gas becomes dangerous when it evaporates out of the water and into people's homes, where it can become flammable. It can also suffocate those who breathe it. According to the Agency for Toxic Substances and Disease Registry, a part of the U.S. Department of Health and Human Services, as the concentration of gas increases it can cause headaches, then nausea, brain damage, and eventually death."

Abrahm Lustgarten. "Colorado Study Links Methane in Water to Drilling." ProPublica, April 22, 2009. www.propublica.org/article/colorado-study-links-methane-in-water-drilling-422.

ly populated that it does not contain a single traffic stoplight. But by early 2011 state environmental officials were urging the county's children and elderly residents to stay indoors due to poor air quality. "Folks who live near the gas fields in the western part of this outdoorsy state are complaining of watery eyes, shortness of breath and bloody noses because of ozone levels that have exceeded what people in L.A. and other major cities wheeze through on their worst pollution days,"[48] wrote journalist Mead Gruver. "'It is scary to me personally,' said a local resident who manages a snowmobile dealership. "I never would have guessed in a million years you would have that kind of danger here [in western Wyoming]."[49]

In early 2012 researchers from the Colorado School of Public Health at the University of Colorado–Denver released a study that found a clear relationship between air pollution from fracking sites and serious and chronic health problems for people living in

A protester at a farm in New York uses a skeleton figure to emphasize concerns about the health implications of pollution caused by fracking operations.

nearby areas. They found that exposure to toxic chemicals released into the air during the fracking process contributed to headaches, difficulty breathing, and sore throats among nearby residents. In addition, the report's authors said that their data, gathered over the course of three years, pointed to "higher cancer risks for residents living nearer to the wells as compared to those residing further [away]. Benzene is the major contributor to lifetime excess cancer risk from both scenarios."[50]

The natural gas industry criticized the Colorado study. The West Slope Colorado Oil and Gas Association, for example, stated, "This report lacks the necessary supportive data and proper context,"[51] and claimed that shale gas operators emphasized the capture of potentially dangerous natural gas emissions at all of their wells.

Reassessing Fracking's Impact on Global Warming

When hydraulic fracturing first emerged as a tool of the natural gas industry, many climate scientists and environmentalists hailed it as a welcome development. They believed that if the United States and other countries that use a lot of energy used more natural gas, they would be less reliant on oil and coal, which generate large amounts of carbon-based greenhouse gases responsible for global warming. As the industry developed, however, some environmentalists reassessed fracking's impact. "If we could convert our coal-fired power plants to natural gas (which in most cases is not that hard to do), carbon emissions would drop," wrote McKibben. "But it's actually not that simple. . . . If even a little bit leaks out to the atmosphere in the drilling process, gas can cause even more global warming than coal."[52]

Several environmental studies on the total impact of shale gas production have deepened the anxiety of public health advocates and green groups on this subject. A 2011 study released by Cornell University suggested, for example, that if the impact of methane leakage into the atmosphere from gas wells is combined "with the thousands of truck trips required to frack every single well, . . . natural gas obtained by fracking is actually *worse* than drilling for oil and possibly even coal mining in terms of greenhouse-gas production."[53]

Biologist/environmentalist and fracking critic Sandra Steingraber agrees. As she stated: "[Natural gas is] the Dr. Jekyll and Mr. Hyde of fossil fuels. When burned, natural gas generates only half the greenhouse gases of coal, but when it escapes into the atmosphere as unburned methane, it's one of the most powerful greenhouse gases of them all—twenty times more powerful than carbon dioxide at trapping heat and with the stamina to persist nine to fifteen years."[54] Some environmental groups and energy experts also express concern that if the United States and other nations devote the bulk of their time, effort, and money to natural gas development, they will stop investing in solar power, wind power, and other renewable energy sources that do not generate greenhouse gases.

The debate over fracking's potential positive or negative impacts on global climate change is by no means over. Scientists continue to study the issue, and some environmental organizations still hold out hope that natural gas will emerge as a valuable weapon in the fight against global warming. But as McKibben observed, "Fracked gas is not as clear a winner in this fight as many had originally assumed."[55]

FRACKING IN THE TWENTY-FIRST CENTURY

As the United States and other countries look for ways to meet their energy needs in the twenty-first century, most observers expect the debate over the wisdom of fracking for natural gas to intensify further. Supporters continue to claim that fracking has a bright future and that it can lift the world to new heights of energy security and economic prosperity. Critics are united in asserting that fracking poses serious dangers to the environment and public health, and they worry about the consequences of its expansion into China, Europe, Argentina, and other gas-rich parts of the world. Divisions exist even within the anti-fracking camp, though. Some opponents want an outright ban on hydraulic fracturing. Others believe that fracking can still be a net benefit, provided that tough new regulations are imposed to protect air, water, wildlife, and public health.

An Evolving Business Environment

Fracking's near-term future in the United States will depend on the choices of a wide array of lawmakers, regulators, and voters in the months and years to come. In the Northeast, for example, officials are weighing whether to end moratoriums on shale gas drilling. Such bans have long been enforced by both the state of New York and the Delaware River Basin Commission, a regional water resource management agency that includes the governors of Delaware, New Jersey, New York, and Pennsylvania.

The natural gas industry has urged that these moratoriums be lifted, and it has been joined by other businesses and by property owners who would like to lease their lands for gas exploration and extraction. Anti-fracking forces in the scientific, environmental, and public health communities, though, have warned state officials against lifting the bans. A representative of the anti-fracking group CREDO Action even declared that the political future and legacy of New York governor Andrew Cuomo rides on whether he upholds the state's moratorium on fracking. "He could go down in history as the governor who poisoned New York state's water supply,"[56] said the spokesperson.

Cuomo has indicated that he will not make a decision until the state's Department of Environmental Conservation finishes a study of the issue. Many observers, though, expect Cuomo to sign off eventually on a partial lifting of the moratorium that would pave the way for fracking in New York's economically depressed southern counties. The Delaware River Basin Commission, meanwhile, is still carrying out environmental impact

A protester at an anti-fracking rally in Albany, New York, in 2012 makes a personal appeal to Governor Andrew Cuomo to uphold the state's moratorium on shale gas drilling.

studies on natural gas exploration in the Delaware River watershed. The commission has stated that no fracking will be allowed in the basin until it has put detailed gas drilling regulations in place.

Debating Federal Oversight of Fracking

People on both sides of the debate over fracking are also waiting anxiously to see whether the industry becomes subject to increased federal regulation from the EPA. In late 2011 the EPA released a study indicating that underground aquifers used by residents of Pavilion, Wyoming, for drinking water had been polluted as a direct result of hydraulic fracturing. The study marked the first time that federal authorities explicitly blamed groundwater contamination on seepage from fracked shale deposits.

WHO PAYS?

"Given the vast scope of fracking we will see, and the fact that fracking involves the release of toxic chemicals and generates potentially hazardous wastes, we must assume that there will be sites and natural resources in need of remediation. And so the question inevitably will arise—who will pay to clean up the mess?" —Northwestern University environmental law professor David A. Dana

David A. Dana. "There Goes Paradise." *Chicago Tribune*, June 21, 2012. http://articles. chicagotribune.com/2012-06-21/news/ct-perspec-0621-fracking-20120621_1_frack ing-gasland-drinking-water.

The Pavilion findings were released in the midst of a separate, ongoing EPA examination of fracking's impact on America's water resources. The results of this study are expected to be released at the end of 2012, and both advocates and opponents of fracking agree that they could have a major impact on the natural gas industry. The Sierra Club, Natural Resources Defense Council, Wilderness Society, and other major environmental organizations have all expressed hope that the study will convince the EPA to approve significant new antipollution regulations on hydraulic fracturing activities across the nation.

A resident of Pavilion, Wyoming, holds a jar of contaminated water from his well in 2009. Two years later, the EPA determined that the contamination was the result of fracking operations in the area.

The natural gas industry claims that new federal rules are unnecessary and would be economically destructive. "Enacting national regulations for these activities would not only be duplicative and costly for states to implement, it would indicate a fundamental disregard for states' expertise in managing their

A Future of Super Fracking?

Companies that provide fracking services to the natural gas industry are working furiously to develop innovative new methods of extracting shale gas. One area of emphasis is to find ways to create longer and deeper cracks in shale rock formations in order to extract even more gas—to "superfrack," in other words. "I want to crack the rock across as much of the reservoir as I can," explained one fracking expert. "That's the Holy Grail."

Some companies are investing in technology to improve the fracking capacity and flexibility of the wells themselves. Others are exploring blasting techniques that would reach deeper into shale formations than ever before. Industry giants like Halliburton are also continually refining their methods and equipment in order to reduce the wastewater they generate, limit the size of their well pads, and better focus on particularly promising gas zones.

Quoted in David Wethe. "Like Fracking? You'll Love 'Super Fracking.'" *Bloomberg Businessweek*, January 19, 2012. www.businessweek.com/magazine/like-fracking-youll-love-super-fracking-01192012.html#p1.

own natural resources," declared the industry group Institute for Energy Research. "Up to 80 percent of natural gas wells drilled in the next decade will require hydraulic fracturing; one can only imagine the bureaucratic nightmare that would ensue upon granting the federal government . . . even more oversight of each operation."[57]

The International Energy Agency, however, is urging corporations and nations involved in shale gas exploration and extraction to be more receptive to new environmental and public health regulations. The agency's executive director, Maria Van der Hoeven, explained:

> On one hand, we must avoid excessive regulation which chokes innovation and threatens the viability of the industry. . . . [But] there are also legitimate public concerns about its environmental and social impacts. . . . We must be sure that safeguards and rules are effective—and include proper oversight mechanisms. But not only that—politicians and the public must be reassured of that ef-

fectiveness. Otherwise, we are likely to see a backlash against unconventional extraction methods, and blanket bans [on fracking].[58]

New Rules Proposed for Fracking on Federal Lands

As opponents and advocates of fracking await the results of the EPA study, they are also assessing the impact of other environmental rules. In April 2012 the EPA handed down new regulations designed to reduce emissions of smog-forming air pollution from fracking operations and other drilling activities. Since many gas companies already voluntarily followed these new regulations, they did not cause much of a stir within the gas industry. At around the same time, though, gas companies and

A drilling rig from a fracking operation stands amid the mountains of Rifle, Colorado. The industry is facing increased environmental regulation, particularly for operations conducted on federal lands.

their supporters expressed unhappiness with new fracking rules proposed by the U.S. Department of the Interior (DOI).

The DOI is the federal agency responsible for managing most public lands and natural resources in the United States. Since about 14 percent of all natural gas production in America comes from public lands (and about 90 percent of those wells are fracked), DOI regulations have a significant impact on the natural gas industry. The 2012 DOI regulations will require frackers seeking drilling permits on public land to submit much more detailed information about their well operations, including their plans for safely disposing of all fracking wastewater. The gas companies will also have to submit test results showing the integrity of their well seals before they begin fracking. The DOI rules also stipulate that once the fracking procedure is complete, drillers will have to publicly disclose all the chemicals present in their fracking fluid.

A CHALLENGE TO FRACKING CRITICS

"Fracturing . . . benefits the economy, has kept natural gas prices at historic lows, and reduces our reliance on foreign energy supplies. Opponents of fracturing should be asked how they intend to duplicate these results . . . and whether their position is in the best interests of lower-income Americans who benefit from affordable energy." —Journalist Christopher Helman, who covers energy issues for *Forbes* magazine

Christopher Helman. "Why Anti-fracking Groups Are Shifting Their Story from Water to Air Quality." *Forbes*, May 8, 2012. www.forbes.com/sites/energysource/2012/05/08 /why-anti-fracking-groups-are-shifting-their-story-from-water-to-air-quality.

The gas industry complains that these new rules will make fracking more expensive and hinder economic growth. Some environmental groups, however, believe that the new regulations should have been even stronger. Sierra Club executive director Michael Brune, for example, stated, "It is deeply disappointing that fracking on sensitive public lands has been considered at all," considering that the industry is "infamous for exploiting loopholes to operate with no regard for the health of our lands

A Possible Link Between Fracking and Earthquakes

The chief public relations problems that the natural gas industry has faced since the emergence of fracking have concerned the issues of water contamination and air quality. Since 2010, though, a potentially explosive new environmental issue has emerged: some scientists now believe that fracking operations are causing earthquakes in some seismically sensitive regions of the world. The threat does not come from fracking wells themselves, however. Rather, seismologists say that the earthquakes are caused by even deeper wells that are used to store fracking wastewater. Some of these wastewater wells, they explain, are disturbing sensitive fault lines located deep underground in so-called basement rock.

Hydraulic fracturing operations have been blamed for dozens of minor earthquakes in the United States since 2009, as well as moderate-strength ones in Arkansas, Ohio, Oklahoma, and Virginia. In November 2011 a British gas company publicly acknowledged that its drilling activities were the probable cause of two small earthquakes in England. One year later, researchers with the U.S. Geological Survey published a study that they said documented a clear linkage between fracking operations and increased earth tremors.

Despite these findings, many scientists and industry experts believe that increased seismic activity related to fracking is unlikely to derail the practice. They acknowledge, though, that the industry will face a tremendous public backlash if a major earthquake that causes death or extensive property damage is ever linked to hydraulic fracturing.

A well in Youngstown, Ohio, used to store fracking wastewater sits idle in January 2012 after being linked to small earthquakes in the area.

or the health of our families." He added, however, that the organization fully expected the Obama administration "to implement the toughest safeguards possible to rein in irresponsible practices and protect our public spaces."[59]

Future regulation of fracking and other activities related to the oil, coal, and natural gas industries also will likely depend to some degree on American voters. Both opponents and supporters of fracking agree that if Republicans control the White House and Congress, they will remove or loosen regulations on fracking that Democrats generally favor.

Natural Gas Development Around the World

Either way, the U.S. natural gas boom is expected to continue for the foreseeable future. One factor in this continued growth is America's vast shale gas fields. In 2012 the Energy Information Administration estimated that the United States held 862 trillion cubic feet (24.4 trillion cu. m) of shale gas reserves, second only to China. Another factor is an expected continued rise in global demand for natural gas. In 2012 the energy giant ExxonMobil predicted that by 2025, natural gas would surpass coal as the planet's second-largest energy source (behind oil). The company also forecast a 60 percent increase in worldwide production of natural gas by 2040.

Many industry analysts and scientists believe, however, that the United States will lose its status as the world's leading gas producer over the next few decades. Energy-hungry China has even larger reserves of shale gas—29.3 million acre feet (36.1 trillion cu. m), according to Energy Information Administration estimates—and the Chinese government is investing heavily in fracking operations, gas pipelines, and other aspects of natural gas development. Other parts of the world have big shale gas reserves, too, including Argentina and Australia.

Europe is another region that frequently gets mentioned as a future center of fracking activity. Gas companies have found promising shale gas reserves in England, and eastern European nations like Poland and Ukraine with significant shale gas fields are openly encouraging foreign energy companies to do business there. In other parts of Europe, though, the shale gas

This fracking operation in Lancashire, England, is one of many that England has approved to tap its shale gas reserves.

industry has received a hostile reception. Concerns about frack-ing's potential for polluting groundwater supplies and surface waterways have led both France and Bulgaria to ban hydraulic fracturing.

European skepticism about fracking is high for other reasons as well. Europe has a much higher population density than the United States, which makes it tougher for fracking companies to find suitable well sites. Even more importantly, European civil-ians do not have the same economic incentives to allow fracking on their land that American civilians do. "In the U.S., people can own the mineral rights below their land, which means energy companies have to pay property owners to drill on their land to make up for the inconvenience," explained *Time* reporter Bry-an Walsh. "But in Europe the government controls the mineral rights even on private land, so property owners endure the pain of drilling without enjoying the profits."[60]

What the Future Holds

No one knows exactly what the natural gas industry will look like ten, twenty, or fifty years from now. Whatever form it takes, most observers believe that hydraulic fracturing will still be a centerpiece of the industry. Fracking operations may look a lot different in a decade or two, however. Fracking companies are exploring new technologies that could bring about a new era of "superfracking," and future regulations could shape industry behavior and practices in all sorts of ways.

Shale gas "is a great resource," according to energy expert Daniel Yergin. "[It] is the biggest energy innovation probably in the last 30 years that we've seen. But it has to be [extracted] in a way that is both environmentally responsible and also acceptable to the public."[61] Bill Chameides, who serves as dean of Duke University's School of the Environment, offered an even more succinct summary of an energy future that is likely to be heavily influenced by fracking of shale gas. "Shale gas is here to stay, a resource that will be exploited," he said. "So we'd better get it right."[62]

Introduction: The Promise and Peril of Fracking

1. Brad Plumer. "Why Regulating Gas Fracking Could Be Cheaper than the Alternatives." *Wonkblog, Washington Post*, May 29, 2012. www.washingtonpost.com/blogs/ezra-klein /post/why-fracking-regulations-could-be-cheaper-than-no -regulations-at-all/2012/05/29/gJQAfcUKzU_blog.html.

2. Sheril Kirshenbaum. "Americans Not So Familiar with Hydraulic Fracturing." *Culture of Science* (blog), June 20, 2012. www.cultureofscience.com/2012/06/20/americans-not-so -familiar-with-hydraulic-fracturing.

Chapter 1: The Origins and Development of Fracking

3. Quoted in George Constable and Bob Somerville. *A Century of Innovation: Twenty Engineering Achievements That Transformed Our Lives*. Washington, DC: National Academies Press, 2003. www.greatachievements.org/?id=2988.

4. Paul Roberts. *The End of Oil: On the Edge of a Perilous New World*. New York: Houghton Mifflin, 2004, p. 41.

5. Seamus McGraw. *The End of Country*. New York: Random House, 2011, p. 42.

6. Daniel Yergin. *The Prize: The Epic Quest for Oil, Money and Power*. Rev. ed. New York: Free Press, 2008, p. 411.

7. Quoted in Yergin. *The Prize*, p. 361.

8. Bill McKibben. "Why Not Frack?" *New York Review of Books*, March 8, 2012. www.nybooks.com/articles/archives/2012 /mar/08/why-not-frack.

9. Quoted in Mark Rowe. "On Shaky Ground." *Geographical*, April 2012, p. 32.

10. Robert F. Kennedy Jr. "How to End America's Deadly Coal Addiction." *Financial Times*, July 19, 2009. www.ft

.com/cms/s/0/58ec3258-748b-11de-8ad5-00144feabdc0
.html#axzz238fvvVOu.

11. Robert F. Kennedy Jr. "Statement Regarding Hydraulic Fracturing," March 7, 2012. www.riverkeeper.org/news-events
/news/safeguard-drinking-water/frackinggas-drilling/robert
-f-kennedy-jr%E2%80%99s-march-7-2012-statement
-regarding-hydraulic-fracturing.

12. Quoted in Jonathan Fahey. "No Energy Industry Backing for
the Word 'Fracking.'" *Wall Street Journal*, January 27, 2012.
http://online.wsj.com/article/AP98dcc66f92764ea488
c3211a338ce7c6.html.

Chapter 2: How Modern Fracking Works

13. Quoted in Mark Koba. "Fracking: How It Works, Where
It's Done; The Well." CNBC, June 20, 2012. www.cnbc
.com/id/47834540/Fracking_How_It_Works_Where_It_s
_Done?slide=3.

14. Quoted in Koba. "Fracking."

15. Sarita Rose Upadhyay and Min Bu. "Visual Impacts of Nat-
ural Gas Drilling in the Marcellus Shale Region." Cornell
University, Department of City and Regional Planning, Fall
2010, p. 2. http://cce.cornell.edu/EnergyClimateChange
/NaturalGasDev/Documents/City%20and%20Regional%20
Planning%20Student%20Papers/CRP5072_Visual%20
Impact_Final%20Report.pdf.

16. *Economist*. "Landscape with Well: Despite Its Poor Image,
Fracking Causes Little Mess or Disruption," July 14, 2012.
www.economist.com/node/21558462.

17. Marcellus Shale Coalition. *Recommended Practices for Site
Planning, Development, and Restoration*, April 26, 2012.
http://marcelluscoalition.org/wp-content/uploads/2012/04
/Site-Planning-Development-and-Restoration.pdf.

Chapter 3: The Benefits of Fracking

18. Robin Millican. "Hydraulic Fracturing—Is It Safe?" Institute
for Energy Research, May 3, 2011. www.instituteforenergy
research.org/2011/05/03/hydraulic-fracturing-is-it-safe.

19. Dan Vergano. "Natural Gas Gold Rush: Is Your State Next?" *USA Today*, July 2, 2012. www.usatoday.com/news/nation /story/2012-05-29/fracking-environment-gas/55845708/1.

20. Quoted in Jonathan Weisman. "In Western Pennsylvania, an Energy Boom Not Visibly Stifled." *New York Times*, June 20, 2012. www.nytimes.com/2012/06/21/us/an-energy-boom -in-western-pennsylvania.html?_r=2&pagewanted=all.

21. McGraw. *The End of Country*, p. 7.

22. Quoted in *Morning Edition*. "Daniel Yergin Examines America's 'Quest' for Energy." NPR, September 20, 2011. www .npr.org/2011/09/20/140606249/daniel-yergin-examines -americas-quest-for-energy.

23. Timothy J. Considine, Robert W. Watson, and Nicholas B. Considine. "The Economic Opportunities of Shale Energy Development." *Energy Policy & the Environment Report*, Center for Energy Policy and the Environment at the Manhattan Institute, May 2011, p. 17. www.manhattan-institute.org /pdf/eper_09.pdf.

24. Quoted in Kevin D. Williamson. "The Truth About Fracking: What the Protesters Don't Know." *National Review*, February 20, 2012, p. 26.

25. EnergyFromShale.org. "Groundwater Protection." www.en ergyfromshale.org/ground-water-protection.

26. Seamus McGraw. "Drilling Down: Fact vs. Fiction in the Great Fracking Debate." *Popular Mechanics*, September 2011, p. 104.

27. Andrew C. Revkin. "'Gasland' Filmmaker Takes on Cuomo and 'Dot.FlatEarth.'" *Dot Earth* (blog). *New York Times*, June 28, 2012. http://dotearth.blogs.nytimes.com/2012/06/28 /gasland-filmmaker-takes-on-cuomo-and-dot-earth.

28. Ian Urbina. "Regulation Lax as Gas Wells' Tainted Water Hits Rivers." *New York Times*, February 26, 2011. www.ny times.com/2011/02/27/us/27gas.html?pagewanted=all.

29. Quoted in Terrence Henry. "How the Natural Gas Industry Is Responding to the EPA Fracking Contamination Report." *StateImpact: Texas, Reporting on Power, Policy and the*

Planet, December 13, 2011. http://stateimpact.npr.org/texas/2011/12/13/industry-responds-to-epa-fracking-contamination-report.

30. Kevin Begos. "Experts: Some Fracking Critics Use Bad Science." Associated Press, July 22, 2012. http://bigstory.ap.org/article/experts-some-fracking-critics-use-bad-science.

31. Quoted in *Gasland* (blog). "Josh Fox, NYS Breast Cancer Network, Dr. Sandra Steingraber Respond to AP Article, 'Experts: Some Fracking Critics Use Bad Science' by Kevin Begos," July 24, 2012. www.gaslandthemovie.com/blog/?p=119.

32. McGraw. "Drilling Down," p. 104.

33. Ronald Bailey. "Natural Gas Flip-Flop." *Reason*, August–September 2011, p. 46.

Chapter 4: The Drawbacks of Fracking

34. Josh Fox and Barbara Arrindell. "Fracking Is Hardly Leakproof." *Albany (NY) Times Union*, June 20, 2012. www.timesunion.com/opinion/article/Fracking-is-hardly-leakproof-3646458.php.

35. Abrahm Lustgarten and ProPublica. "Are Fracking Wastewater Wells Poisoning the Ground Beneath Our Feet?" *Scientific American*, June 21, 2012. www.scientificamerican.com/article.cfm?id=are-fracking-wastewater-wells-poisoning-ground-beneath-our-feeth.

36. Quoted in Lustgarten and ProPublica. " Are Fracking Wastewater Wells Poisoning the Ground Beneath Our Feet?"

37. Abrahm Lustgarten. "So, Is Dimock's Water Really Safe to Drink?" ProPublica, March 20, 2012. www.propublica.org/article/so-is-dimocks-water-really-safe-to-drink.

38. Quoted in McKibben. "Why Not Frack?"

39. U.S. House of Representatives, Committee on Energy and Commerce, Minority Staff. *Chemicals Used in Hydraulic Fracturing*, April 2011. http://democrats.energycommerce.house.gov/sites/default/files/documents/Hydraulic%20Fracturing%20Report%204.18.11.pdf.

40. Amy Mall. "New NRDC Analysis: State Fracking Disclosure Laws Fall Painfully Short." *Switchboard* (blog), Natural Resources Defense Council, July 26, 2012. http://switchboard .nrdc.org/blogs/amall/new_nrdc_analysis_state_fracki .html.

41. Ian Urbina. "Regulation Lax as Gas Wells' Tainted Water Hits Rivers." *New York Times*, February 26, 2011. www.ny times.com/2011/02/27/us/27gas.html?pagewanted=all.

42. Urbina. "Regulation Lax as Gas Wells' Tainted Water Hits Rivers."

43. American Rivers. "Hydrofracturing and the Impact on Your Clean Water." www.americanrivers.org/initiatives/pollution /energy-pollution.

44. Gary Wockner. "Will Fracking Destroy Colorado's Rivers?" *Huffington Post*, March 19, 2012. www.huffingtonpost.com /gary-wockner/colorado-fracking_b_1358822.html.

45. Wockner. "Will Fracking Destroy Colorado's Rivers?"

46. Wockner. "Will Fracking Destroy Colorado's Rivers?"

47. McKibben. "Why Not Frack?"

48. Mead Gruver. "Wyoming Air Pollution Worse than Los Angeles Due to Gas Drilling." *Huffington Post*, March 8, 2011. www.huffingtonpost.com/2011/03/08/wyoming-ait -pollution-gas-drilling_n_833027.html.

49. Quoted in Gruver. "Wyoming Air Pollution Worse than Los Angeles Due to Gas Drilling."

50. "Study Shows Air Emissions Near Fracking Sites May Pose Health Risk." University of Colorado, Denver Newsroom, March 19, 2012. www.ucdenver.edu/about/newsroom /newsreleases/Pages/health-impacts-of-fracking-emissions .aspx.

51. David Ludlam. "The McKenzie Report—Regarding Human Health Risk Assessment of Air Emissions from Development of Unconventional Natural Gas Resources." West Slope Colorado Oil and Gas Association, March 20, 2012. www .wscoga.org/node/78.

52. McKibben. "Why Not Frack?"

53. Quoted in Christopher Bateman. "A Colossal Fracking Mess." *Vanity Fair*, June 21, 2010. www.vanityfair.com/business /features/2010/06/fracking-in-pennsylvania-201006.

54. Sandra Steingraber. "The Whole Fracking Enchilada." *Orion*, September/October 2010. www.orionmagazine.org /index.php/articles/article/5839.

55. McKibben. "Why Not Frack?"

Chapter 5: Fracking in the Twenty-First Century

56. Quoted in Inae Oh. "New York Fracking Protest Urges Cuomo to Ban Controversial Drilling." *Huffington Post*, August 22, 2012. www.huffingtonpost.com/2012/08/22/new-york -fracking-protest-cuomo-photos_n_1822575.html.

57. Millican. "Hydraulic Fracturing—Is It Safe?"

58. Quoted in International Energy Agency. "Legitimate Public Concerns over Fracking Must Be Addressed." IEA Newsroom and Events, August 20, 2012. www.iea.org/news roomandevents/news/2012/august/name,30653,en.html.

59. Quoted in Sierra Club. "Sierra Club Statement on the Bureau of Land Management's Proposal for Federal Land Fracking," May 4, 2012. http://action.sierraclub.org/site /MessageViewer?em_id=237901.0&dlv_id=0.

60. Bryan Walsh. "The Golden Age: Could Europe and China's Fracking Forays Remake Global Energy?" *Time*, May 22, 2012, pp. 47–48.

61. Quoted in *Morning Edition*. "Daniel Yergin Examines America's 'Quest' for Energy."

62. Bill Chameides. "Minds Meet on Shale Gas, Fracking." *The Green Grok* (blog), January 10, 2012. www.nicholas.duke .edu/thegreengrok/frackingworkshop.

DISCUSSION QUESTIONS

Chapter 1: The Origins and Development of Fracking

1. Why did natural gas remain such a minor energy source for so many years?
2. What factors did environmentalists emphasize in supporting shale gas over coal?
3. Are the gas industry's objections to the term *fracking* legitimate? Why or why not?

Chapter 2: How Modern Fracking Works

1. What functions does slickwater serve in the fracking process?
2. Why is site remediation such an important part of fracking operations?
3. What measures do fracking companies take to protect drinking water supplies?

Chapter 3: The Benefits of Fracking

1. Do you find arguments that fracking will increase America's energy independence to be convincing? Why or why not?
2. In what ways do fracking operations increase job opportunities?
3. How does the natural gas industry defend itself against charges that its activities endanger public health and the environment?

Chapter 4: The Drawbacks of Fracking

1. Should the fracking experience of residents of Dimock, Pennsylvania, receive as much attention as it has? Explain.
2. Should fracking companies be forced to reveal the exact chemicals that they use to create their slickwater?

3. Do you agree with industry's contention that more environmental regulation of fracking would greatly reduce its economic benefits? Why or why not?

Chapter 5: Fracking in the Twenty-First Century

1. After considering the arguments for and against fracking, do you think that New York State should lift its ban on the practice? Explain you answer.

2. Explain how negative news stories and poor publicity could limit the growth of fracking in the years ahead.

3. List three ways in which your life could be directly affected if fracking came to the county where you live.

Damascus Citizens for Sustainability (DCS)

PO Box 147
Milanville, PA 18443

The DCS is a grassroots nonprofit organization that is a leader in efforts to keep fracking operations out of the Delaware River basin. The DCS also believes that fracking should be banned across the country.

Earthworks Oil and Gas Accountability Project

1612 K St. NW, Ste. 808
Washington, DC 20006
Phone: (202) 887-1872
Website: www.earthworksaction.org

The Earthworks Oil and Gas Accountability Project is a national nonprofit organization dedicated to protecting people and the environment from the effects of irresponsible energy development. The organization's Oil and Gas Accountability Project collaborates with local and state groups to push for oil and gas industry regulations and reforms that will protect human health and ecosystems in regions experiencing energy development.

Energy In Depth (EID)

1201 Fifteenth St. NW, Ste. 300
Washington, DC 20005
Phone: (202) 587-4200
Website: www.energyindepth.org

The EID was created by the Independent Petroleum Association of America in 2009 as a research, education, and lobbying initiative designed to increase public support for shale gas extraction through fracking and other techniques. A special focus of the EID has been to counter criticisms of the natural gas industry from documentary filmmaker Josh Fox, the creator of *Gasland*.

Marcellus Shale Coalition (MSC)
24 Summit Park Dr.
Pittsburgh, PA 15275
Phone: (412) 706-5160
Website: www.marcelluscoalition.org

The MSC was founded in 2008 by an assortment of companies involved in the natural gas industry. Its mission is to provide policy makers, regulators, the media, and members of the public with information on the positive impacts of natural gas production on families, businesses, and communities.

Natural Resources Defense Council (NRDC)
40 W. Twentieth St.
New York, NY 10011
Phone: (212) 727-2700
Website: www.nrdc.org

The NRDC is one of the largest and most influential environmental protection organizations in the United States. NRDC activities include a wide range of campaigns and activities related to energy development and use, including hydraulic fracturing.

Books and Periodicals

Saul Elbein. "Here's the Drill." *Texas Monthly*, October 2011. http://m.texasmonthly.com/id/15991/Energy/#part1. This article tells the story of a Texas couple who find their lives turned upside down by fracking.

Seamus McGraw. *The End of Country*. New York: Random House, 2011. This book examines the explosive growth of fracking in Pennsylvania from the perspective of a man whose family is directly affected by the shale gas boom.

Seamus McGraw. "Is Fracking Safe? The Top 10 Controversial Claims About Natural Gas Drilling." *Popular Mechanics*, 2011. www.popularmechanics.com/science/energy/coal-oil-gas /top-10-myths-about-natural-gas-drilling-6386593#slide-1. This slideshow from *Popular Mechanics* seeks to clarify the truth behind some of the most pressing controversies surrounding fracking and natural gas exploration.

Bill McKibben. "Why Not Frack?" *New York Review of Books*, March 8, 2012. www.nybooks.com/articles/archives/2012 /mar/08/why-not-frack. This article from one of America's most prominent environmental writers summarizes the primary fears about hydraulic fracturing.

Ian Urbina. Drilling Down series, *New York Times*, 2011–2012. www.nytimes.com/interactive/us/DRILLING_DOWN_SE RIES.html. Beginning in early 2011, *New York Times* reporter Ian Urbina published a series of critical articles about various aspects of the fracking industry in the United States, including negative environmental and public health impacts. The series, which is ongoing, is available in its entirety on this website.

Websites

Energy In Depth (www.energyindepth.org). This website, which includes a wide assortment of multimedia offerings and links, provides a good overview of pro-fracking arguments. Energy In Depth was created by the Independent Petroleum Association of America to garner support for natural gas development.

Fracking: Gas Drilling's Environmental Threat, ProPublica (www.propublica.org/series/fracking). The independent investigative journalism organization ProPublica has issued a wide range of reports and stories on hydraulic fracturing. These works, which focus on environmental and public health dangers associated with fracking, are collected at this website.

Fracking: What Is It, and Is It Safe?, *PBS NewsHour* (www.pbs.org/newshour/rundown/2012/08/fracking-is-it-safe.html). This website provides an informative overview of the debate over fracking, as well as numerous links to videos and articles that detail the arguments of the pro-fracking and anti-fracking camps.

Gasland: **A Film by Josh Fox** (www.gaslandthemovie.com). This website maintained by documentary filmmaker Josh Fox contains comprehensive information on his anti-fracking *Gasland* movie and provides educational materials about hydraulic fracturing and its negative environmental and public health impacts.

"Shaleionaires," *60 Minutes* (www.cbsnews.com/video/watch/?id=7054210n). In November 2010 the CBS News program *60 Minutes* broadcast a segment on the shale gas boom in Pennsylvania. This website provides the complete video of that piece, called "Shaleionaires," as well as a transcript of the broadcast and additional bonus footage that was not included in the original program.

INDEX

A
Agency for Toxic Substances and Disease Registry, 65
Air pollution, 49, 64–66
American Petroleum Institute, 20, 37–38
Aquifers
contamination of, 46, 70
threat of fracking to, 52–55
Arab oil embargo (1973), 15

B
Battlestar Galactica (TV program), 23
Bush, George W./Bush administration, 17, *18*, 50

C
Cabot Oil and Gas Corporation, 55
Cheney, Dick, 17
China, shale gas potential in, 76
Coal
environmental impacts of, 19
share of total U.S. power production from, 50
Coal mines/mining, 31, *31*
Colorado Oil and Gas Conservation Commission (COGCC), 45

Colorado School of Public Health (University of Colorado–Denver), 65–66
Cornell University, 67
Cuomo, Andrew, 69

D
Delaware River Basin Commission, 69–70
Department of Energy, U.S. (DOE), 37
Department of the Interior, U.S. (DOI), 74
Dimock (PA), backlash against fracking in, 55
DOE (Department of Energy, U.S.), 37
DOI (Department of the Interior, U.S.), 74
Drilling rig(s), *36*, *73*

E
Earthquakes, link between fracking and, 7, 75
Employment, from fracking, 38, 40
Energy Information Administration, U.S., 35–36, 76
Energy Policy Act (2005), 17–18

EnergyFromShale (website), 43–44

Environmental Protection Agency, U.S. (EPA), 46, 63, 73

Europe, skepticism about fracking in, 76–77

ExxonMobil, 76

F

Fossil fuels, U.S. reliance on, 58

Fox, Josh, 42, 45

Fracking (hydraulic fracturing)
  bans on, 68
  controversy over term, 21–24
  debate over federal oversight of, 70–73
  development of, 13–15, 72
  earthquakes linked to, 75
  economic benefits of, 28, 38–41
  on federal lands, 73–74, 76
  future of, 78
  process of, 27–28, 29, 30
  public's awareness of, 7
  status of natural gas and, 6

G

Gasland (film), 42, 45

Geological Survey, U.S., 75

Global warming
  natural gas as tool in fight against, 49–51
  reassessing fracking's impact on, 66–67

Ground Water Protection Council, 35

H

Halliburton Loophole, 17–19, 56

Health risks
  of fracking, 47
  for fracking workers, 33
  of methane, 65

Hydraulic fracturing. *See* Fracking

I

Ickes, Harold, 12

Industrial Revolution, 8–9

Institute for Energy Research, 36

International Energy Agency, 72

K

Kennedy, Robert F., Jr., 19, 21

M

Marcellus Center for Outreach and Research (Penn State University), 20

Marcellus Shale Coalition, 34

Marcellus Shale formation, 31
  economic benefits of fracking in, 20
  estimates of recoverable gas in, 37

Media, portrayal of fracking in, 48

Methane, 44

in drinking water, 55
as greenhouse gas, 67
public health danger posed
    by, 65
Monongahela River, 59

N
National Academy of
    Engineering, 9
National Institute for
    Occupational Safety and
    Health, U.S. (NIOSH), 33
National Petroleum Council, 20,
    38
Natural gas, 10–12
    decline in cost of, 41
    fracking and status of, 6,
        16–17
    global development of, 76
    percentage of production from
        federal lands, 74
    See also Shale gas
Natural Resources Defense
    Council (NRDC), 57, 70
NIOSH (National Institute for
    Occupational Safety and
    Health, U.S.), 33
Nitroglycerin, 15
NRDC (Natural Resources
    Defense Council), 57, 70

O
Obama, Barack/Obama
    administration, 20, 50
Occupational Safety and Health
    Administration, U.S. (OSHA),
    33

Oil, 15
    decline in U.S. reserves of,
        12–13

P
Pavilion (WY), contamination
    of groundwater in, 46, 70
Pipelines, 12, *13*, 16

R
Remediation/restoration, of
    fracking sites, 32–34
Roosevelt, Franklin D., 12

S
Safe Drinking Water Act (1974),
    56
Sand, role in fracking, 22
Shale gas
    early support by
        environmentalists of, 19
    growth in production of,
        20
    main deposits of, *17*
    U.S. reserves of, 76
    See also Natural gas
Slickwater, 28, 30
    secrecy over chemicals in,
        56–58
    use of sand in, 22
Stanolind Oil and Gas
    Corporation, 14

U
United States
    decline of oil reserves in,
        12–13

percentage of power produced
  from coal in, 50
reliance on fossil fuels in, 58
shale gas production in, 20
shale gas reserves of, 76
University of Texas, 7
Urbina, Ian, 42

W
Wastewater, 20
  inadequate treatment of,
    42–43
  radioactivity levels in, 43,
    46–47, 60

Water
  amounts used in fracking,
    25, 48–49, 62–64
  contamination of, 42–43,
    45, 58–62
  See also Slickwater
Wells/well pad(s), 26
  drilling/casing of, 25–27
  home, contamination by
    fracking operations,
    45
  horizontal drilling of, 27
West Slope Colorado Oil
  and Gas Association, 66

PICTURE CREDITS

Cover: © Shuli Hallak/Terra/Corbis

© Amy Sussman/Corbis, 53

© AP Images/Amy Sancetta, 75

© AP Images/Casper Star-Tribune/Kerry Huller, 71

© AP Images/David Duprey, 61

© AP Images/David Zalubowski, 73

© AP Images/Keith Srakocic, 42, 59

© AP Images/Orlin Wagner, 39

© AP Images/Ralph Wilson, 21

© Bettman/CORBIS, 13

© David Grossman/Alamy, 23

© FLPA/Alamy, 77

© Gale/Cengage Learning, 17, 29

© Jason Janik/Bloomberg via Getty Images, 47

© J. G. Domke/Alamy, 26

© Les Stone/Corbis, 45, 50, 57, 62, 66, 69

© Mandel Ngan/AFP/Getty Images, 18

© Niday Picture Library/Alamy, 31

© Spirit of America/Shutterstock.com, 11

© Trevor Collens/Alamy, 36

© Vespasian/Alamy, 32

ABOUT THE AUTHOR

Kevin Hillstrom is an independent scholar who has written numerous books on environmental issues, U.S. politics and policy, and American history.